Bipolar Me

Janet Coburn

Eliezer Tristan Publishing
Portland, OR

All rights reserved

Copyright © 2018

No part of this book may be reproduced or transmitted in any form or by any means, electronic or mechanical, including photocopying, recording, or by any information storage or retrieval system, permitted by law. For information contact Eliezer Tristan Publishing, Portland, OR.

Cover design by Aaron Smith

For Dan,
always

Table of Contents

Introduction 9
Author's Notes 11
Chapter One – Brain Games **13**
Me and My Brain: A Story of Love and
    Dysfunction 15
Mind Like a Steel Trap 17
A Little Bit of This, A Little Bit of That 19
My Brain, My Books 21
The Teen in My Head 23
Creativity and the Bipolar Brain 27
Sensation in the Brain 31
Senses and Sensitivity 35
Chapter Two – Symptoms Galore **39**
Bipolar Basics for the Newly Diagnosed 41
The Pluses and Minuses of Highs and Lows ... 47
Brain Hamsters, Stomach Badger 51
When Anxiety Attacks 53
Dental Health and Mental Health 55
Does Depression Hurt? 57
Stress Plus 59
How I Function (When I Do) 61
The Sky is Falling! 63
The Railroad Spike in My Temple 65
Where's the Anger? 69
I Want to Go Home to Bed with My Kitties 71
Managing My Anger 73
Self-Care and Sleep 77
Stuffing Your Feelings in a Box 81
The Seven Wonders of the Bipolar World 83
Chapter Three – The Med-Go-Round **85**
Crazy Pills 87

Saving Face, or You Can Die From That? 91
How Psychotropics Helped Me Get My Brain
    Back 93
The Overwhelming Problem 99
Trial and Error 101
Music Charms the Troubled Mind 103
Things that Work – Sometimes 107
Does "Natural" Treatment Work for
    Depression? 111
Support and Non-Support 115
Am I Ready to Stop Therapy? 119
Running Out of Drugs 123
Chapter Four – Family Matters **127**
Bipolars, Rollercoasters and Sex............................129
A Portrait of the Blogger as a Young Bipolar 133
A Bipolar Child 135
A Grain of Salt 139
Mini-Meltdowns and Many Meltdowns...............141
Family Matters...145
A Mother? Me? 147
Mr. Fix-It...149
Taking Turns..151
How a Cat Helped Me Stay Sane 153
Chapter Five – Heavy Weather **157**
On the Inside..159
Suffering and Train Wrecks 161
Cutters...163
Self-Harm Revisited 167
Missing Friends 171
The Myth of Closure 175
What Was I Thinking? 179
The Wrong Life..183
The Week of Living Alone 187
Reaching the End of My Cope 191
Struggles and Tears...193

What Bipolar Disorder Has Cost Me 197
The Comfort That Remains 201
Chapter Six – Swings Go Both Ways **205**
The Hypomanic Blogger 207
Ack! Ack! 209
From Panicky to Manicky 211
Maybe Another Manic Monday 213
The Fragility of Hypomania 215
Out of the House, At Last 219
I Got Away Successfully! 223
Looking Back – But How Far? 225
Beware the Mental Health Meme! 229
Chapter Seven – On the Upside **233**
Cookie Theory 235
Misery and Math 237
Confessions of a Crazy Cat Lady 239
Work Hacks 243
In Defense of the Armadillo 247
Bipolar Me vs. Disney World 249
Those Science Fiction Crazies 253
The Depression Diet 257
Brain vs. Brain 261
Chapter Eight – The Social Whirl **263**
A Closet of Disguises 265
Surviving High School (and Reunions) 267
How I Learned a Few Social Skills 269
I Have This Friend… 273
I'm Not Brave – I'm Stubborn 275
Social, But Spoonless 277
I May Have Miscounted My Spoons 281
A Crowd-Hater at a Conference 285
The Therapeutic Hug 289
Chapter Nine – Issues: My Take **293**
A Tattoo is for Life… 295
Those Who Will Not See 299

The Answer to Bullying..303
Owning My Bullying 307
Yes, I Am Crazy. Thanks for Asking. 311
My Second Mental Health Tattoo 313
Read Your Way to Sanity 317
Diagnosis and Dickinson..321
Is My Cat Bipolar?..325
Response to the Dalai Lama.....................................329
I Chose Fat Over Misery...333
Who's a Spoonie? 337
Chapter Ten – Society, Sickness and Sanity 339
What Is Sanity? 341
On the Street...345
All in Our Heads 347
Why Do They Do This? And Why Do We Allow
    It? 351
Fun's Fun. Until It Isn't...355
Trigger Warning: Trigger Warning 357
Is Bipolar Disorder an "Invisible Illness?"............361
We've Got Demons in Our Heads 365
New Hope for Mental Illness...................................369
More "News" About Mental Health 375
The Scientific Tease 381

Introduction

BACK WHEN my diagnosis was depression and anxiety, I secretly envied the manic-depressives, as they were called. At least if I had a manic phase, I thought, I could get something *done*.

Then I met Kerri, who was bipolar. She was not stabilized on medication to say the least. My envy lasted through her ambitious plans to make identical green velvet Christmas dresses for her three daughters, and vanished when I saw her tear them apart, recut them, start over, change her mind multiple times. You can write the ending to this one. There were no dresses, not by Christmas and not ever.

Kerri was riding the roller coaster (perhaps the most common metaphor for bipolar disorder) the peaks and troughs, swooping crashes, anticipatory climbs, stomach-clenching vertigo, and, for some, an abrupt stop at the end.

Type 2 bipolar, which my most recent psychiatrist diagnosed me with, is not like that. I never got the manic jags of exaltation and excess that typically go with type 1 bipolar disorder. I mostly didn't even get the brief flurries of purpose and mini-jags of elation called hypomania that can accompany bipolar 2. Instead, those symptoms came out sideways as anxiety. I know it's hard to picture being apathetic, despairing, and anxious all at the same time but I was for weeks, months, even years at a time. It's no way to live, and some people choose not to.

The heights of the mountain are frightening. The depths of the pit are unrelenting. The challenge is to stumble down and struggle up until you find level ground.

Author's Notes

I AM NOT a psychiatrist, a psychologist, a psychotherapist, or even a psychology major. I am a person with bipolar disorder and these are my experiences. Nothing in this book should be taken as medical advice. I am not recommending any of the medications I discuss. Your Mileage May Vary.

In this book, you will often see me refer to "Spoon Theory." I didn't invent it, but I've found it enormously useful in describing the effects of bipolar disorder to people with no experience of the condition. Here is the origin: http://www.butyoudontlooksick.com/articles/written-by-christine/the-spoon-theory/. It started as a metaphor to explain "invisible illnesses" and why people who have them are limited in what they can do.

Here's a quick synopsis: Every day you get a certain number of spoons. Every day the number of spoons is different. You use them to perform everyday tasks that most people think nothing of, things like getting out of bed, taking a shower, getting dressed, finding something to eat, fixing that something, and all that is without even leaving the house. Some days that's all the spoons you have and when you've used up your spoons, that's it.

Other days you can manage to do all that and leave the house, go to work, run errands, and assorted other normal activities. But for those of us who have chronic illnesses, such days are few and far between.

You hear depressed people talk of not being able to get out of bed, and for the most part that's caused by lack of spoons. I am usually notoriously low on spoons. My husband now understands Spoon Theory and we use it as common shorthand for "I've hit the wall" or "That's all I can handle right now."

This is the way I remember events and conversations happening. Other people involved may remember them differently. I can't say they are wrong, especially given how much my disorder, my medications, and the intervening time have affected my memory. If they want to write books from their point of view, they are welcome to do so. But these are my perceptions, presented as honestly as I can. Some names have been changed to protect the privacy and self-regard of various persons.

Chapter One: Brain Games

Me and My Brain: A Story of Love and Dysfunction • Mind Like a Steel Trap • A Little Bit of This, A Little Bit of That • My Brain, My Books • The Teen in My Head • Creativity and the Bipolar Brain • Sensation in the Brain • Senses and Sensitivity

Me and My Brain: A Story of Love and Dysfunction

AS THEY SAY, of all the things I've lost, I miss my mind the most. Or anyway, a properly functioning brain.

I love my brain, despite all the trouble it's given me. For many years I thought it was the only measure of my worth, the only thing about me that made me special, the only thing that I could truly rely on.

I reveled in learning, in thinking, in reading, in questioning, in contemplating, in discovering. My body was not dependable; my brain was.

Little did I know the biochemical pitfalls that were waiting for me. Little did I know that my brain was ill. Disordered. Unbalanced. At the very least, uncooperative.

For instance, my brain decided other people were always pointing and laughing at me. Sometimes they were, of course, but that paranoia became my baseline assumption. Shrinks call that "ideas of reference." I just called it life.

My brain played back for me every socially awkward or embarrassing thing I ever did, randomly and at the worst possible moments.

My brain made me cry at the stupidest times, at an upbeat sitcom theme song, when someone mentioned foreign travel, when opening boxes from the garage, when thinking about my college years, or at birthday parties. Whenever I was confronted with how damaged I am.

My brain had irrational thoughts. Bad thoughts. Self harm. Worse.

Eventually my brain refused to let me live any kind of a normal life, to go out, talk to people, care for my house or my pets or myself, or even read, which was once the greatest joy of my life.

    But my brain also worked just well enough to send me looking for the help I needed. I've gotten back parts of who I was and what my mind was. And for that, I'm grateful. Even with it disorderly and uncooperative, it's still the best part of me.

Mind Like a Steel Trap

RUSTY. UNHINGED. Not good for trapping things. Especially memories.

That's not quite true. I have that uncanny ability that all depressed people seem to have to remember every stupid, clumsy, embarrassing thing I've ever done as well as every trauma. It's like a mental recorder that stores them up, then plays them at random moments. Or maybe not so random. Maybe just when I think I'm doing okay.

The memories can be as traumatic as the time other children threw rocks at me or as trivial as the time one person asked for a glass of water and I gave it to someone else.

Unfortunately, the recording feature only works for bad memories. Most of the good ones are MIA. I don't remember huge chunks of my childhood except as stories that family members have told me. I don't really know if the memories are mine or theirs. And I'm scared to compare notes.

My theory about these childhood memory deficits, and to tell the truth, all the way through those of my teens and early twenties, is that when you are profoundly depressed, memories don't imprint the way they're supposed to. Whatever synapses and neurochemicals are involved in memory making are out of whack. I'm also afraid to do the simple Googling required to find out whether this is even a plausible theory. If it's not, I don't think I want to know. I have an explanation that makes sense to me, and the memories won't come back if I learn my theory is wrong.

Later in life, medication has helped controlled the depression and the other effects of bipolar 2. But if I thought my memory was going to function properly, I was wrong. Some of the drugs left me with a memory like Swiss cheese. My memory lapses seem more random now. Good things, bad things, neutral things, all disappear into the Swamp of Unavailability. Sometimes they are embarrassing, like forgetting a friend's father had died and asking how he was. Other times they are more distressing, only scraps left of trips I've taken. Sometimes they're heart-searing, a total non-recall of a never-to-be-repeated sexual encounter.

Good and bad, gone.

"Oh, yes," said the doctor. "That drug will do that. You can stop taking it now."

I guess I'm lucky. If I'd had electroshock, as my doctor once recommended, my memory would probably be as raggedy as old underwear. And about as useful.

A Little Bit of This, A Little Bit of That

I'VE NOTICED that a lot of my friends who have a psychiatric diagnosis display at least minor symptoms of other conditions as well. Depression with a side of Tourette's. Bipolar with a helping of OCD. OCD with a smidge of anxiety disorder. PTSD with all the above.

The symptoms of the secondary problem are usually not severe enough to warrant a second diagnosis and a separate treatment regimen. Most likely the add-ons are noticeable only to the person who has them, or possibly to very close friends.

I don't exclude myself. I have little rituals that help get me through the day, a certain order I do things in. I have a couple of words or phrases I mutter under my breath to keep me centered when I am stressed. "Kittens" for mild stress and "jumping" for more than mild. I suppose that if I ever get into kinky sex, I could use those as my "safe words."

Do these mini-disorders ever grow into major ones? I don't know. They could be coping mechanisms or side effects of medication or routine habits or personality traits. Mostly I think I should ignore them until they start causing problems with my life. My husband, formerly a certified addiction counselor, says when drinking or drugs start *causing* problems in finances, work, relationships, legal matters, and so on, that's how to tell when drinking or drugs they have become a problem.

For now, they're just little quirks, reminders that my brain has an alternative wiring scheme.

My Brain, My Books

IT USED TO BE that I could never be found without a book within arm's reach. I had a purse book, a nightstand book, a bathroom book, and a car book at the very least.

Now that I have an e-reader, I have hundreds of books with me everywhere I go, but I'm doing a lot less reading.

I think it's due to my lack of concentration. Whether that's the disorder or the meds I couldn't say.

I do know that when I was in the depths of my most recent breakdown I barely read at all. I watched moronic reality shows like *Trading Spouses* on the theory that these people's lives were bigger train-wrecks than mine. I watched cooking shows because they were calming. Not that I ever tried any of the recipes.

During an earlier meltdown, I tried to watch sitcoms but the relentlessly upbeat theme songs made me weep.

Now I must hoard my concentration like I hoard my spoons. I am fortunate enough to be able to work freelance from home. But it's the kind of work that sometimes has deadlines. On days when I can force myself to work, I can concentrate for about 2-1/2 to three hours at a spell. Some days I have to do two sessions like that with a nap in between, if a deadline is approaching rapidly.

But when it comes to non-work activities, I can usually only concentrate for an hour at the most. Sometimes I try hard so that I can watch a movie. I usually stick to hour-long shows at most.

Reading takes concentration too. I do a lot of my reading in bed at night. I know you're not supposed to do that because it keeps you from falling asleep but it's a life-long habit.

My mind flitters, the brain hamsters and sometimes the stomach badgers stir, and I find myself several pages along with no idea what happened. At that point, my need for distraction and my attention span collide and I have to find something moderately absorbing but short-term to do. It's a good thing I have some games on my e-reader.

Reading has been one of the great joys of my life since I was four. It bothers me that I no longer have the ability to immerse myself in it the way I used to.

But, like so many other things, it's something I'm having to learn to live with. Or without.

The Teen in My Head

THERE IS SOMEONE else living inside my brain.

I don't have Dissociative Identity Disorder. I just have another me who pipes up from time to time. And man, she can be annoying!

She's 14 years old, and she doesn't have a name. I don't know when I acquired her, but I do know when she acts up.

She's the one who frets when a friend doesn't answer my message. When he does, she squees, "He noticed me! He noticed me!" She's the one who wants to buy ridiculous, useless, but amusing things. She makes me eat that extra chocolate cookie, then frets about getting fat and pimply. She's the one who is hooked on all the stupid internet games.

I've heard the theory that everyone has a mental age that they get stuck at. No matter how old they get, they always picture themselves at that age. Mine is somewhere between 28 and 34. So how did I end up with a 14-year-old?

My theory about her existence is that she is there to try to do what I never did when I was 14, all the regular teen-age angst and frivolous stuff: mad crushes and pouting, self-obsession and discovering her sexuality, in-jokes with best friends and trying out fingernail polish.

When I was 14, I did none of that. I was in a prolonged downward mood swing, made worse by puberty and the horrors of junior high school. I wrote depressing poetry and read French existentialists. If they had had hipsters back then I suppose I would have been one.

When I feel her popping up in the back of my skull, most of the time I put her in a box and sit on the lid. It's scary to let her take over. She's rapid-cycling, impulsive, and, worst of all, unmedicated. (I don't know why my meds don't affect her, but there you are, they don't.)

Once in a while I let her out of the box. I let her enjoy some mad crushes, as long as she doesn't do anything about them. I let her buy things that cost $20 or less. One time I let her talk me into fake fingernails. I let her have some of the fun that I never had at that age.

The thing is, I don't know if this is a me thing, a female thing, or a bipolar thing.

I know I'm not completely alone in having a teen ride-along. I do know a man with dissociative identity disorder who has an alter that is a teen girl. I could tell when she was out because she giggled a lot and bought junk food. A friend of mine who has suffered from depression also has a 14-year-old in her head. She has given her teen a name: Innie Me. Hers behaves a lot like mine.

I also don't know whether having a teen living in my head is a good thing or a bad thing. It could be good, because it does give me access to the feelings and experiences I never had as an actual teen. My teen is better than I am at having fun.

On the other hand, I know it would be a bad thing if I let her have her way all the time. She needs that box and I need to sit on the lid. The trick is knowing when and how and for how long to let her out.

On an episode of *Scrubs*, one character remarks that no matter how old a woman gets she always has an insecure 14-year-old inside her. I suppose that men experience similar phenomena. Most people are said to have an inner child. I think my husband's inner child is usually about seven or 11, tops.

Certainly, my teen is insecure. There's no question about that. But she's also enthusiastic, engaged, and energetic as well as moody, dramatic, and confused. I think she may be related to the hypomanic part of myself, although I'm also sure some of my fits of apparently reasonless weeping have been caused by her acting up.

My therapist knows about my 14-year-old. We have discussed her and her behavior and her moods several times. Dr. B. has never expressed surprise or shock or puzzlement at the idea. She does think it's good that I'm learning to sit on the box lid when I need to. We've talked less about when it's a good time to let her out. That's something I still need to work on.

I guess I'll have to learn to live with my 14-year-old, because I don't think she's going away anytime soon. And I don't think I really want her to.

Creativity and the Bipolar Brain

Sun or shade
feel or know
safe or strayed
stall or flow

Thought or whim
drought or rain
sink or swim
heart or brain

Stop or start
bound or free
light or dark
bipolar me

I HAVE A LOT of friends who are creative, writers, musicians, singers, woodworkers, knitters, and other artists and craftspeople. I also have a lot of friends who have assorted mental or emotional disorders: depression, bipolar, PTSD, OCD, and probably many more that I don't know about. In many cases, the creative and disordered categories overlap.

Common wisdom holds that there is a link between creativity and madness. Look at Van Gogh, for example. People have spent years debating what specific disorder he may have had, but nearly everyone agrees that he had *something*. The question is, would he have been the great artist without the mental or emotional disorder? Or, perhaps, would he have been an even greater artist if his brain functioned in a more typical matter? Science so far has given us no answers.

Many creative people realize that their everyday functioning is impaired, but they are reluctant to seek treatment for it. They fear that tampering with their brain or thought processes will somehow inhibit their creativity, somehow make them less than they are in some fundamental way. When you start tampering with brain chemistry, who knows what will happen?

It's a valid concern.

Throughout my life, my brain has been all that I have. My intelligence and creativity were the things I was most proud of. How could I risk losing those simply because I was eternally miserable? The question seems absurd now.

Eventually I decided that I had plenty of brain cells to spare, and that if taking Prozac took away a few of them or lessened their ability, I could live with that. I took up pursuits that are supposed to strengthen the brain just in case. Things like math puzzles, word puzzles, music, and of course writing. Not everything I tried was a success, but I hoped they stretched my "brain muscles."

My experience with that first psychotropic med convinced me that Better Living Through Chemistry is not just Dow's slogan. It turns out that (surprise, surprise) thinking more clearly and feeling more well-adjusted actually empowers one's creativity. My output changed from poems full of young adult angst to creative nonfiction, personal essays, and the occasional short story. I now make my living doing freelance writing and editing, a style of work that I couldn't have made a go of before having my mood disorder treated. The ability to concentrate, to focus, is what enables me to sustain a creative effort.

So, to all those people out there who wonder if they are sabotaging themselves and their creative impulses by seeking treatment, I say you have nothing to lose but your immobility. You have everything to gain: the ability to create, expressing yourself and doing it clearly, and the possibility of creating something truly wonderful.

Sylvia Plath was a poetic genius. But she could have given so much more of her talent and vision to the world if she had not killed herself. Perhaps her poetry, had she been treated for her mood disorder, would not have been as searing and powerful. But, the point is, we will never know. Would she have become more ordinary, or more extraordinary? Dying young hides the answer.

I believe, for me, that psychological treatment, appropriate medication, and more stable moods have expanded my creative process. I try to prove it every week by posting in two blogs. Whether I succeed is for readers to determine.

Have I lost a step? Maybe, but two forward and one back beats the hell out of one forward and two back.

Sensation in the Brain

I KNOW THERE is no physical sensation in the brain. It cannot feel pain. It cannot feel touch. Even in a car accident when the brain sloshes from side to side, bashing against the sides of the skull, the brain sustains injuries, but feels nothing.

That notwithstanding, twice in my life I have felt physical sensations in my brain. Or at least what felt like sensations.

The first time was at the dentist.

He brought in a traveling anesthesiologist so that I could be unconscious during the procedure instead of being terrified. My husband was there with me, both to drive and to give moral support.

While the anesthesiologist was putting me under, my husband and the dentist were casually chatting. My husband made a remark and the dentist said, "Oh, she can't hear us now. She's already pretty far under and won't remember a thing."

"I bet she will," my husband replied.

The bet involved giving me a word to try to remember when I awoke. They selected the word *green*.

"You mean like the color of my pants?" I said.

"Yes," the dentist replied. "Green, the color."

Just for the hell of it, as I was sinking into unconsciousness, I silently repeated to myself the word *green* in a slow and steady manner: *green, green, green*. Then the drugs took me under.

An unknown time later I awoke. The dentist asked me, "Is there something you were supposed to remember?"

I shook my head groggily.

As soon as I did, I felt an odd sensation in the back of my brain. It was like a little bubble rising up through liquid. When the bubble reached the surface, it burst and released the word *green*. "Green?" I said uncertainly.

"See?" said my husband. "I told you she would remember."

The other sensation in my brain came about six weeks after beginning a new psychotropic medication. I had gone through a long, miserable time of trying drug after drug after drug , tapering off on one and ramping up on the next, all with only unpleasant effects.

My doctor was ready to recommend electroshock for me. After what may have been two years of trying and failing with different medications, I was ready to take the plunge. I admitted as much in one of my sessions.

"There's one more thing I'd like to try before we do that," said Dr. R. "Here is a prescription for Lamictal."

"Okay," I said. "How does it work?"

"We don't really know," he replied.

This was our standard conversation whenever he prescribed a new drug. I was used to it, but I always asked anyway.

So, I tried it. And felt the usual nothing for almost six weeks. Then one day, in my husband's study while we were talking, I felt it.

It was the physical sensation in the back of my brain of a light switch being flipped. I thought I heard an internal click. When that switch flipped, suddenly something in my brain changed. It remembered how to think and to feel and to not be miserable.

"Oh!" I said. "I remember this. This is the way my brain is supposed to work."

Since then it has kept working often enough that I consider the drug a success.

I know that in both of those cases nothing happened in my brain that caused a physical sensation. Both times, my brain gave me a metaphor for what was happening. In the dentist's office the metaphor was a bubble rising to the surface to explain coming out from under sedation and a little bit of self-hypnosis.

In the case of the drug, the metaphor was the flipping on of a light switch. This time something had changed in my brain, something biochemical. I shouldn't have been able to feel it, but according to my brain, I did.

It seems I have a clever brain. It gave me ways to understand what was happening in terms I could relate to. The fact that I know the brain can have no physical sensations did not matter to my brain.

Human brains are amazing. Sometimes even in a good way.

Senses and Sensitivity

WHEN I WAS a child, I was often told that I was "too sensitive", meaning that I took things too much to heart, especially criticism, taunts, and bullying from other children. It was something that I assumed was innately wrong with me and that I didn't know how to fix.

These days, however, I'm too sensitive to sensory input.

I used to be able to write or read or edit with instrumental music on. I used to be able to hold a conversation while the television was on. I used to be able to drive a car and look at the scenery around me.

Not anymore.

A fan is about all the sound I can handle while I write and sometimes quiet is the only thing that will calm my nerves. I can barely process remarks anyone makes *about* the TV show we're watching. And if I'm driving, I never even notice a deer in a field off to the side of the road. I doubt I would notice a hippopotamus.

Over the years, at least since my last major meltdown, I have had trouble processing more than one sensory signal at a time.

It's not just a matter of focusing too completely on just one thing.

My ability to focus has been a casualty of my bipolar disorder. At my lowest point, I couldn't even read a book, which is something I've been doing since I was three or four. I still can read only one chapter or one magazine article in a sitting.

Now that I'm recovering (thank God and my doctors.), I can concentrate enough to read, write, and edit. What I can't do is separate out multiple sources of information on the way from my senses to my brain. If my husband talks while a TV show is on, it's not just that I can't make sense of what he's saying. I can't process either signal: the TV or him. It's all a jumble.

If I went to cocktail parties, I would be unlikely to have an intelligible conversation because of all the ambient noise and clashing voices. I recently went to a workshop that held a mix-and-mingle event on the first day. Having people chatting all around me was not just distracting, it was almost painful and immobilizing. Focusing on one person at a time was the only way I could get through it.

And forget about Chuck E. Cheese or Cici's Pizza! No. Just no. Video arcades, are you kidding? It's a good thing I have no reason to frequent places like that. When I go to a regular restaurant, I ask not to be seated near any birthday parties or office functions. I wish they had a "no screaming" section for people who can't tolerate families with young children.

I understand that sensory processing difficulties sometimes occur in persons with autism spectrum disorders and ADHD. I have never been diagnosed with an autism spectrum disorder, though I may have manifested Asperger-like traits in my youth and adulthood. I have been told by doctors that I have hyper-sensitive nerves. Is that the same as what I experience? I don't know.

Most of the research and discussion of sensory processing and bipolar disorder occurs in the context of children, though I never noticed such difficulties when I was a child. But just as articles about autistic adults are rare and learning disabilities are forgotten about as soon as a person leaves school, it seems that sensory processing problems in adults also get little attention.

I can't be the only one dealing with this.

As I learn more about my own difficulties and conditions that affect others, there is one conclusion I'm rapidly approaching: neurodivergent is neurodivergent. We may have different diagnoses, but we share so much.

Chapter 2 – Symptoms Galore

Bipolar Basics for the Newly Diagnosed • The Pluses and Minuses of Highs and Lows • Brain Hamsters, Stomach Badgers • When Anxiety Attacks • Dental Health and Mental Health • Does Depression Hurt? • Stress Plus • How I Function (When I Do) • The Sky Is Falling! • The Railroad Spike in My Temple • Where's the Anger? • I Want to Go Home to Bed With My Kitties • Managing My Anger • Self-Care and Sleep • Stuffing Your Feelings in a Box • The Seven Wonders of the Bipolar World

Bipolar Basics for the Newly Diagnosed

IF YOU HAVE recently been diagnosed as bipolar, there are a few basics you should know. You'll likely find them out on your own, but it could take a while.
So, here are some tips.

1. **Being bipolar isn't necessarily a tragedy.** It's a chronic illness. At times it's better, at others, worse. It's not a death sentence and it's treatable. You can still live a full and satisfying life.
2. **You need help.** To live with bipolar disorder, you need a support system. Unfortunately, your friends and family may not be all that supportive. However, there are online support groups. The most important parts of your support system, at least at first, are your psychiatrist and your psychotherapist. I recommend having one of each: a psychiatrist for medication, and a therapist for talk or cognitive behavioral therapy. Find what works for you.
3. **You will most likely need medication.** The odds are good that you will need it for the rest of your life. Don't panic. After all, diabetics need insulin. You may hate taking pills, you may hate the idea that you are dependent on them, you may hate the fact that they remind you of your brain's difficulty functioning. But know that meds will make your brain's functioning less difficult. They are worth the hassle.

4. **Everyone is different.** Everyone's symptoms are slightly different. Everyone's medications are slightly different. Everyone's reactions to their medications are slightly different. A support group can help you with general information, but they cannot tell you what is ultimately best for you. Your particular symptoms and your unique version of bipolar disorder may well require different medications and different amounts than your friends. And you may have different reactions to them. Some pills have no effect at all on one person yet are life-savers for another.
5. **Getting better takes time.** Once you have your diagnosis and your medication, don't expect to feel better quickly. Most medications for bipolar disorder take a while to build up in the body. Six weeks is not unheard of. Then your doctor may assess how well the medication is working and change the dose or even the medication itself. *Then* you may go through another six weeks of waiting for the new dose or drug to take effect. Each case of bipolar disorder requires a medication regimen tailored specifically to the individual, and that often takes some doing.
6. **There are several different types of bipolar disorder.** The two main types are called type 1 and type 2. Type 1 is the classical bipolar disorder, which used to be called manic-depressive illness. Type 2, a more recently identified version of the disorder, often manifests as mostly depression, possibly with hypomania, a less severe version of the ups that accompany bipolar 1. Other forms of

bipolar disorder are rapid cycling, in which one's mood states alter quickly, even within a few hours. Another version of bipolar disorder is called mixed states. Mixed states occur when a person experiences both extremes of emotion at the same time – for instance, depression and irritability, or fatigue despite racing thoughts.

7. **The odds are that you already know someone with bipolar disorder.** or at least some kind of mood disorder. One in four Americans will have a psychiatric or emotional illness at some time during their lives. Because we don't talk about it, though, no one may ever know. Especially when the disorder is treated properly, a person with bipolar illness can function in society and choose whether or not to share the diagnosis with friends and coworkers. Many people choose not to because of the stigma surrounding mental illness. It's a valid choice, but it cuts the bipolar person off from possible support and understanding from others who may share the disorder.

8. **Relationships can be difficult but are not impossible.** Relationships are difficult for everyone. The disorder may make the relationships even more difficult, especially when the family member or loved one or even close friend does not understand the symptoms, the medication, the mood swings, the anxiety or fatigue, or all the other facets of bipolar. The best cure for this is education. However, it may not be possible for a relationship to survive bipolar disorder, just as a relationship may not survive trauma, grief, addiction, infertility, incompatibility, meddling

relatives, infidelity, parenting, or a host of other factors. It may be better to look at all the circumstances surrounding a troubled relationship rather than automatically blaming bipolar disorder for difficulties.

9. **Learn all you can.** Because bipolar disorder is so little understood by the public, because it manifests differently in nearly every case, because a person can be actively suffering or in remission, because a person may have any of the different types of bipolar disorder, because everyone is different – educating yourself and probably those around you is essential. The more you know, the less you'll panic when a symptom you haven't experienced before suddenly hits. Rely on reputable sources. Medical, psychiatric, and psychological websites are usually the best. Support groups can offer much information, but the people in a support group may not be any more well-informed than you are. And there are lots of people selling "miracle cures" that can lure a person away from needed medication and other services.

10. **Keep trying.** It's hard. It's frustrating. It's difficult. It's painful. It's confusing. But bipolar disorder is something you can live with, even something you can rise above. The secret is to keep trying. Keep seeking out therapy and friends who support you. Keep taking your medication, even if you don't want to. (Stopping your medication without advice from your doctor can be dangerous, so don't try that.) Be stubborn. When you feel like giving up, tell yourself that maybe things will

get a little better in the morning. Hang in there. You may not realize it, but there are people who need you in the world, who need you to be functioning and happy, who need you to keep fighting the disorder.

The Pluses and Minuses of Highs and Lows

BIPOLAR DISORDER comes with highs and lows, mania and depression for those who still call it manic-depressive illness. Bipolar 2 comes with plenty of depression (trust me on this), but mania that doesn't reach the heights of regular mania. Hence the term "hypomania" – low mania. Like "hypoglycemia" – low blood sugar.

So, mania. Mania comes with pluses, exuberance, euphoria, ambition, confidence, and other good feelings. It also comes with minuses, risk-taking behaviors that can ruin relationships, careers, finances, lives.

Hypomania, however, is not so extreme. Sometimes you don't even realize that you have hypomania at all, because it comes out sideways, as anxiety. This is what happened to me and is the reason it took me so long to get the proper diagnosis of bipolar type 2.

Recently I have been exploring the realm of hypomania, and I'm here to report that, similar to regular mania, hypomania has its attractions and its drawbacks. And they are intertwined.

On the plus side, I have more energy. More spoons to spend. I can go longer between naps. I have now gotten out of bed, dressed, and out of the house for three days in a row. I can concentrate longer on the books I'm reading and spend more time with my husband and do some actual paying work.

On the minus side, I pay for that energy. It's like borrowing spoons – you can't keep doing it. Sooner or later the spoons have to be replaced. Right before my most recent spurt of energy, I had a need for a nap that turned into a mega-nap, almost six hours. I woke up just in time to get ready for bed. Then I slept at least 10 hours more. It's impossible to schedule these things, so I left the next day open just in case my body and brain decided that was payback day for the three days of activity.

Another plus is that my creative juices flow. I work ahead on blog posts if I know at the end of the month I have a huge commitment that will keep me from writing for my regular Sunday posts. I've also taken steps to spiff up my posts with visuals. And I've been toying with writing a mystery novel.

However, there's a however. The last time I had a creative spurt I almost talked myself into starting two new blogs, for a total of four. I had plenty on my plate already, what with blogs and paying work and trying to find an agent for my hypothetical book and getting ready for a writer's conference. This was no time to start a big new project that could easily devour my time and my ability to do the things I already need and want to do. But I do have a computer file set aside for notes and ideas that flit through my busy brain. Call that file "Later."

And let's not forget anxiety. It's hard to find the pluses there except that anxiety, if properly harnessed, helps me prepare. I suppose it sounds better if I call it anticipation instead of anxiety. Anticipating my upcoming dental work spurred me into putting together the financing for it. Anticipating the writers' workshop allowed me to prep for all the details, wardrobe, business cards, parking, strategies to cope with exhaustion. Things that would make my nerves fray even more at the last minute.

I assume I needn't discuss the minuses of anxiety. Let's just say that for me, they include regrettable and appalling physical symptoms that no one wants to hear about.

Bipolar disorder is often compared to a seesaw, teeter-totter, a swing, or a roller coaster. The ups and downs are with us always. Better to learn to ride this beast rather than let it ride us.

Brain Hamsters, Stomach Badger

I'M SURE YOU ALL are way too familiar with the brain hamsters, those little buggers who spin your wheels whenever you try to fall asleep. It's not a new phenomenon, a new concept, or even a new name for it.

There is, however, another inner animal that has plagued me.

My last full-time job caused me a great deal of anxiety. Monumentally so. My boss left, and I felt I should tell my new boss about my depression (not diagnosed as bipolar yet). She said, "What does that mean?" Uh-oh. My stomach sank, and the badger moved into my stomach.

I missed a lot of time at work dealing with my mother's failing health and finances, in addition to my own. She was blown over by a gust of wind, fell like a plank, and landed on her face. A neighbor sent her kid over: "Go see if she's alive." I had to have the you-can't-live-alone talk with her. Find a nursing home. Figure out how to pay for it. Et cetera.

I could feel the stress in my stomach. A nasty badger, red in tooth and claw, growing daily, snarling more loudly, and threatening to claw its way out, like that scene in *Aliens*.

There was one good thing about the badger. Its presence alerted me that it was time to get the hell out. So, I quit my job to go freelance. And it worked. For a while. I remember feeling happy, feeling free, as I drove on my errands and worked at my own pace and on my own schedule.

Of course, it couldn't last. The badger was only lying low, waiting for another round of disasters to resurrect it. And they came. My, how they came.

Then the badger won. My brain broke. I had the lowest level of depression I can remember since college. It was the sort of depression that doesn't let you get out of bed and makes you cry for no reason. All my emotions were blunted except for sorrow and anxiety. Simple household tasks were beyond me. Bills went unpaid, which only made things worse. My husband took up the slack but I had irrational fits of yelling at him. I was as close to non-functional as I ever care to get. I've been trying to piece my brain back together ever since. Thanks to my support system, my doctors and my medications, I am slowly doing so.

But the badger is waiting. I can feel it stirring, even now.

When Anxiety Attacks

I WAS GROCERY shopping and when I came to the cereal aisle, I found myself light-headed and breathing raggedly.

My husband dropped a knife in the kitchen; I jumped, and all my muscles tightened up.

We were driving down the highway, when suddenly I flung my arms out to the sides and gasped loudly.

In none of these cases was anything wrong, although the incident in the car nearly caused an accident when my husband turned and yelled, "What? What?"

My depression has always been accompanied by anxiety. That's one of the reasons I was given a diagnosis of bipolar disorder, type 2. It seems that, where other people get hypomania, I get anxiety. (There is a thorough explanation of bipolar disorder and anxiety or "mixed states" at http://psycheducation.org/diagnosis/mixed-states/anxiety-and-bipolar-disorder/.)

I have had generalized anxiety, where I have no idea whether anything specific is wrong or whether doom is impending. I have had phobic-type anxiety, where I imagine that any bee in the neighborhood is going to choose to sting me and I freeze up. I have had anxiety reactions to loud noises or sudden movements, where I feel like I'm jumping out of my skin and physically jump. And I've had irrational moments of anxiety, as when I can't sleep because I don't know where I put my passport.

Now that I am relatively well controlled on medication, the various anxieties don't plague me nearly as much. And I've developed coping mechanisms for several of them. For example, when I get anxious in the car on the highway I no longer fling out my arms and gasp. My husband notices my tension and asks if anything would make me feel better. "Drive in the other lane," I say, "and not next to the concrete divider." I take an extra, prescribed Ativan before social events I can't avoid. My husband warns me if he is going to hammer a nail in another room or reassures me that the cat just knocked over a glass.

I still don't know what was going on in the cereal aisle. I thought it might be the imposing wall of large, brightly colored boxes, visual "noise" that seemed to overwhelm me. My therapist at the time said that it was likely that I was just having a random anxiety attack and happened to be in the cereal aisle when it happened. After that I associated the two.

I think the anxiety will always be with me, to some extent, just like depression. My meds make it bearable and my ways of handling them improve, but I don't think I'll ever get used to the fact that there are bees, wasps, and ticks in the world, all of them with a thirst for my blood.

Dental Health and Mental Health

I STILL REMEMBER one of my earliest episodes of panic, which happened in a dentist's waiting room. As I sat in the uncomfortable chair, surrounded by *Highlights for Children* magazines that I had already read, I felt dread moving up my body from my toes. It crept up my legs into my hips and on into my abdomen. I was convinced that when the feeling of terror reached my heart, I would die. I was called into the doctor's office before that happened.

This is a memory I have shared with only one other person before now. Just thinking about it still brings back a visceral body memory of fear.

It really bothers me that some people think that good teeth are a sign of moral superiority. Some other people, like me, are simply born with bad teeth, or at least weak, cavity-prone little tooth buds embedded in our infantile gums. Brush as diligently as we might, we are never going to have pristine white teeth like the people on TV.

While my dental phobia can possibly be attributed to the general pool of my anxiety triggers, there were also some outside factors that contributed to it.

My parents were never good role models for dental health. My mother had had dentures at age 16 and my father chewed tobacco.

There were also bad experiences with blame-and-shame dentists and hygienists, one of whom scraped a bit of tartar off my teeth, stuck it in my face, and asked, "If I put that on a piece of bread, would you eat it?"

I used to loathe the public-school practice of making us chew little purple tablets to see how clean our teeth really were. My teeth were – and still are – considerably crooked, so it was difficult for me to brush in a manner that wouldn't leave glaring purple spots all over my mouth.

My teeth have only gotten crookeder, since my parents were not able to afford orthodontia for me. When and where they grew up, braces were a luxury for the well-to-do; rural children like they were simply did without. By the time my sister and I came along we lived in the suburbs, but braces had never become a priority for my parents compared say to eyeglasses, which were deemed essential.

My last and most recent experience with a dentist was a number of years ago. I don't remember what prompted me to go but I did tell the dentist about my phobia and he was very considerate. I always look for a dentist whose advertising says, "We Cater to Cowards."

The only person in the world who is a worse dental-phobia than I am is my sister. She too had childhood dental issues. Once she even bit a dentist and he slapped her. Needless to say, that experience did not improve her attitude toward dental care.

She is also ultra-sensitive to and afraid of pain, and quite terrified of needles. Even as an adult, she has been known to scream so loudly and lengthily that she has cleared an entire dentist's waiting room. She then sent the dentist a Halloween card that screamed when he opened it.

Still, I am a grown-up. I need to do this from time to time. I cannot convincingly tell myself that waiting will improve the situation. I just have to pick a day for my appointment when my husband is available to take me, and I have had my prescription for Ativan recently refilled. And some Imodium on hand. Just in case.

Does Depression Hurt?

YOU'VE PROBABLY SEEN those commercials where the announcer and the actress playing the part of a depressed person try to answer the question: Does depression hurt?

Once when we saw this commercial, my mother turned to me and asked whether my depression hurt me physically. I had to say yes. I was clear on the fact that physical pain is involved along with the psychological suffering of depression. My head and eyes hurt from all the crying spells. My back hurt from lying in bed all day. I had painful knotted muscles from the anxiety that went with the depression. I had intestinal cramps because my overactive nerves led to irritable bowel syndrome. I had headaches and eye strain from the over-sensitivity to light and noise. And I had the general flu-like malaise that is practically the hallmark of depression. You know the one: every bone and muscle aches, but you can't think why.

Were these aches and pains psychogenic? Undoubtedly some of them were. But others, like the irritable bowel, were all too demonstrably physical phenomena.

The mind and body and soul are inextricably intertwined. We know this to be true. Depression affects them all.

And it hurts.

Stress Plus

MENTAL STRESS plus physical stress equals Stress Plus.

The mind and the body are part of the same system. What affects the one affects the other as well. When the body is stressed, the mind suffers. When the mind is stressed, the body suffers.

When both are stressed, you get Stress Plus.

Here's how it works for people with mental disorders. You feel depressed or immobilized yet don't get up and move around. Your body responds by becoming lethargic and flabby. Your mind responds to that by becoming discouraged and self-blaming. What you have there is a feedback loop.

My body and brain have been going different directions of late. My mood disorder has lessened, and my brain doesn't seem to be trying to kill me at the moment. This is good.

However, my body is experiencing all kinds of unpleasant disorders and sensations. Some like thinning hair, jowls, and weakened eyesight are simply functions of aging. This does not make them any easier to deal with. They are wrapped up in my self-confidence, my sexuality, my identity, how others perceive me, how congruent my self-image is with reality.

Stress symptoms have affected me since junior high. I developed a tic in which my chin would jerk up and to the left, making it hard for me (or anyone sitting behind me) to study. My doctor put me on Valium, which stopped the tic, but I'm sure did no good for my then-undiagnosed bipolar disorder.

Other physical ailments and disorders are the result of specific events or diseases. I have a bad back, which required two operations, the second because I irrationally thought it would be a good idea to ride an Arabian horse bareback. The experience has left me with nerve damage in my left toes (idiopathic radiculopathy, they call it) and an unsteady gait that sometimes necessitates the use of a cane for balance. It doesn't make me look or feel any younger.

Also, my hands shake. My neurologist called this an "essential tremor," which means it's caused by nothing in particular. He noticed that I often sit with my hands folded in my lap to call less attention to it. Between this and my balance issues, sometimes I stagger and shake like an old street rummy. God bless the friend who once told me I had a long way to go before looking like a street rummy. It was nice to hear, no matter what my brain tells me.

When my brain was acting up the worst, it also gave me the worst physical symptoms. My reflexes were hypersensitive and that included the reflex that empties my bowels. Just imagine the literal shitstorm I created in the bathroom of a bookstore one day. Then imagine how much of my self-esteem got flushed along with the rolls of toilet paper I used to try to clean it up. Imagine the humiliation of telling a store clerk, "Someone's been very sick in the bathroom and you probably need to send a janitor." I'm sure she knew it was me, because of how embarrassed and sickly I must have looked, but we both pretended that I was simply informing her that an accident had occurred.

All these conditions make me not want to go out amongst people, which adds to the isolation that my bipolar disorder already exacerbates. And when I don't get out, my body doesn't get moving, and I become even more immobilized, both physically and mentally.

Like I said, a vicious circle of Stress Plus.

How I Function (When I Do)

HIGH-FUNCTIONING and low-functioning are terms we use to tell how adept we are at navigating everyday life in the real world. Usually, thought, it's not so clear-cut.

I recently was involved in an online discussion. I probably should have been doing something else at the time, but it caught my interest and I jumped in.

It was, or at least became, about getting up, getting dressed, and doing the work or art or whatever. One person stated that she worked at home, but she needed to get out of her pajamas and get into regular clothes as a signal and reminder to herself that it was time to work.

I work at home too, and when I can make myself do the work, I do it in my pajamas. I reserve getting dressed for when I need to get outside, and that's maybe three or four times a month. Pulling myself together that way takes much effort that I need to invest in doing the work.

So, am I high-functioning or low-functioning? Yes.

We also discussed Dale Carnegie's admonition, "ACT enthusiastic and you'll BE enthusiastic." This advice comes in various forms. Fake it till you make it. You get good at what you practice.

It doesn't work that way for me. I can pull myself together for a limited time on the phone, talking to a client, for example. I can fake it for that long. In my pajamas. A few months ago, I had to drive to a face-to-face, multi-person business meeting. Altogether, about a half a day. By the time I got home, I was not just fried but extra-crispy. Even the next day, I was too exhausted to do much more than get out of bed. It did not result in my being any more pulled-together thereafter.

I was high-functioning for half a day and low- to non-functioning for a day and a half.

I suspect that most of us go bouncing back and forth between high- and low-functioning, with an occasional pause in the middle. It probably goes with the mood swings.

There are high-functioning activities I can (sometimes) do, earn money and blog, for example. There are also ones that I used to be able to do, but now can't: cope with taxes, travel abroad or on business, tolerate crowds. And there are things I can do for a limited time or with help like grocery shop or cook a little. Also, there are things I can do, but not as well as I did before my brain broke: solve puzzles, analyze, concentrate.

I suppose you could count napping as something I can do better now. I am a truly high-functioning napper. Not much of an accomplishment, maybe, but it beats the hell out of insomnia!

The Sky Is Falling!

IF CATASTROPHIZING were a power source, I could light up Chicago. Good thing it burns nerve endings instead of fossil fuels. I wish it burned fossil fuels instead of nerve endings.

The last couple of weeks have seen a lot of anxiety and catastrophizing. I hardly ever get to enjoy the rush of hypomania because in me it comes out sideways as anxiety. I also have a third-degree black belt in catastrophizing.

Both have gotten a workout lately, since a cyst was discovered in my left breast.

I checked my usual sources: Mayo Clinic website and a friend who is a biologist and had a lumpectomy. The consensus was that I had only the remotest chance of the anomaly turning out to be anything really dire.

Do you think that stopped my catastrophizing?

Hell, no!

Let's see, what could happen next?

They could have stuck a needle in my breast to aspirate fluid and get a sample for the lab.

If the results were worse, I could have been scheduled for a lumpectomy. There was extra anxiety on this one because my friend almost had a mastectomy instead of a lumpectomy when the surgeon started making the wrong incision. An operating room tech noticed, saving the day and the breast.

And of course, my anxiety told me that a mastectomy could be in my future, either on purpose or accidentally, I suppose. My mother had a mastectomy, which added extra oomph to the catastrophizing.

A mastectomy would suck for oh-so-many reasons: cancer, surgery, body image issues.

Also, I would keep falling over to the right. And before the operation I'd have to take my breast on a farewell tour for all its friends and admirers.

Maybe worst of all, I would have to put up with all the pinkness and positivity. Not to denigrate this strategy for those who find it helpful, but I am not that person. Anyone with my brain chemistry is not going to respond to slogans and cheerleading and daily affirmations.

Barbara Ehrenreich has written about this phenomenon in *Bright-Sided: How the Relentless Promotion of Positive Thinking Has Undermined America*. Apparently, many breast cancer survivors feel they must get something positive from the experience, appreciating life and family more and so on.

We've come a long way from Betty Rollins's *First, You Cry*. Now it seems like we're never supposed to.

The anticlimactic but welcome result came soon: Everything was OK. I just need to keep up with yearly mammograms.

What a relief! Now I could move on to the next thing that needed angsting about: the work I wasn't able to do while I was catastrophizing.

The Railroad Spike in My Temple

IT WAS THE Year of Living with Rex, and for me that meant dangerously. I was undiagnosed and unmedicated, except for wine. I had already been through an episode of cutting. I was clueless and stubborn, isolated and emotionally abused. Tired to my soul and trying to claw my way through my last year of college and a relationship that has affected me to this day.

Then the pain started. Without warning, I would feel a railroad spike being driven through my right temple. It was blinding, all-consuming, and lasted for as much as 30 minutes straight, sometimes. If I was lucky, it was only a few seconds. I was seldom lucky.

I didn't know anything that would make it better. All I could do was lie down and weep until it went away.

As this continued, the fear grew in me that I had something dire, like a brain tumor. In addition to my major depressive episode, I was living with massive anxiety.

I don't know how I made it through my senior year. I don't know how I made it through the train wreck I was living.

But here's how I made it through the railroad spike.

Actually it was kind of amusing, if you weren't me and it wasn't happening to you. I went to a neurologist who took one look at me and said, "I can give you any test you want, but I'll tell you what it is right now. Your jaw is crooked."

It was Temporomandibular Joint (TMJ) syndrome. And this was before it got trendy and over-diagnosed, the way gluten sensitivity is now.

My jaw was indeed as crooked as could be. When the doctor put his fingertips on my jaw and asked me to open my mouth, we could both feel it slipping sideways. I've been told it feels like my jaw is going to fall off in the doctor's hands. It made clicking and cracking noises that I had somehow never noticed, and occasionally seemed to get stuck briefly.

How did this explain the railroad spike? When I was anxious, my jaw muscles would clench – and since my jaw was crooked, they would tighten up unevenly, causing much pain.

"What can you do for it?" I asked.

"We could break your jaw and put it back together, but there's no guarantee that would work," he said. (This was in the '70s. I believe treatments have improved since then.)

While I contemplated whether I really wanted to have a surgically broken jaw (I did not), he gave me a prescription to calm my anxiety, so the muscles wouldn't tighten up and trigger the pain spasms.

Good ol' Valium.

Now I was officially medicated with benzos and self-medicated with wine. It did take down the anxiety but plunged me even further into the depression. And I was still living with academic pressure, isolation, no psychiatric diagnosis. And Rex.

I finished up the year, grabbed my diploma, and lit out for my home state as fast as I possibly could. Rex threatened to send the police after me if I took my things while he wasn't home to supervise and prevent theft of any of his goods. Fine, I thought. Just let him try. I was across two state lines before he got home from work. No, geographic cures don't work, but sometimes retreating to a safer place can help.

So, all in all, a truly rotten experience. But did I have a psychiatric problem? After all, a crooked jaw is a decidedly, visibly, diagnosably physical ailment.

Of course I did! The crooked jaw was just one component of my condition. The anxiety was another, a big, huge, whopping one. After all, I'd had a crooked jaw my entire life, and it never sent me railroad spikes until that year. And the depression made it all harder to see and to get away from.

If you ever needed proof the mind and the body are so intertwined that you can hardly tell one from the other, there it is. Physical problem + psychological problem = pain, of both sorts. Good luck trying to sort the two out.

Where's the Anger?

DEPRESSION USED TO BE defined as anger turned inward. Now we consider depression to be a biochemical imbalance in the brain. At least that's the current thought, as the pendulum swings back and forth between brain and mind.

There is a case to be made, though, that anger is at least one component of depression. And that anger may indeed be turned inward.

Take, for example, the anger you may feel when a loved one doesn't understand what depression makes you go through, or when a coworker says something clueless and cruel. These are incidents that can make you justifiably angry.

It's all too easy to turn that anger inward. You say to yourself I'm crazy or I'm broken or I'm damaged and it's no wonder they don't understand. Maybe they're right. Maybe most people can just cheer up and I'm defective because I can't. These thoughts, in addition to prompting anger, are likely to depress a depressed person even more.

When anger masquerades as depression, it becomes difficult to recognize the anger for what it is. After a difficult relationship ended, badly, I was unable to see that I was indeed angry. I could have sworn that I wasn't. In fact, I told people that I wasn't angry. It took a long time for me to recognize and acknowledge that anger. By then it was too late to do much about it, except work through it with my therapist. But that's all right, because that's what I needed to do with the anger anyway. I'm at that awkward age when I can be tried as an adult.

So, while I don't think that depression is caused by anger turned inward, I do believe that depression can cause you to internalize anger and beat yourself up for things that you can't control, like your brain.

Depression makes a hash out of feelings. Is it anger? Is it pain? Is it loneliness? Is it despair? The answer, usually, is one from column A and two from column B.

I Want to Go Home to Bed with My Kitties

Kittens.
Jumping.
I want to go home to bed with my kitties.

THESE ARE MY mantras. Or something.

I repeat these phrases under my breath. At least I think it's under my breath. I have at times walked out of a restroom stall to see people looking at me strangely.

My husband says they are "grounding statements," though I understand proper grounding statements are usually more like an affirmation: "I am safe." "I can handle this." "I am a good person." How I ended up with mine I don't quite know.

I do know that I mutter or say them when I am anxious. "Kittens" indicates a general level of anxiety, while "jumping" is reserved for increased levels. "I want to go home to bed with my kitties" is an all-encompassing statement of stress or dissatisfaction, and the only one that I can say nearly out loud around people with only mild looks of incomprehension.

A very few people who know me well are used to this phenomenon and even have responses. When I say, "kittens," my friend Leslie says, "puppies," and my husband says, "Do you like them?" When I say, "jumping," he says, "up and down?" and my friend Robbin says, "You must really be nervous." My husband occasionally joins me in a chorus of "I want to go home to bed with my kitties." The extended version is "I want to go home. I want to go to bed. I want my kitties." The short form is "Home. Bed. Kitties."

I know that I use these vocalizations a lot when I have anticipatory anxiety, or after a protracted spell of having to be competent, social, and appropriate. I say them a lot in my car, or after coming home from braving the outside world. In a crowded, noisy space like a restaurant, I say them in a very matter-of-fact manner, as if I'm having a conversation with my husband.

I can accept the idea that they are non-standard grounding statements. What I know they're not are "clang associations," even though these can be associated with bipolar disorder. The psychotic kind. Which I do not have.

The National Mental Health Association says, "People with obsessive-compulsive disorder try to cope with anxiety by repeating words or phrases."

Fair enough. I do have a few OCD-like traits.

But to me the grounding statements explanation makes the most sense. I would argue that for me, home, bed, and kitties are all things that remind me of safety and bring me comfort. How jumping fits in, I'm not sure, except that I have hyperactive nerves and do a fair amount of jumping. But it certainly isn't associated with safety or comfort. Quite the opposite, in fact.

Speaking of kitten therapy (which I was, sort of), a recent *New York Times* story (http://mobile.nytimes.com/2015/08/16/fashion/how-a-kitten-eased-my-partners-depression.html?referrer&_r=0) was a personal account of how a kitten helped make a man's depression better.

I can testify to the truth of that. Cats or kittens have stayed up with me through bouts of insomnia, snuggled when I needed touch, purred when I needed quiet, demanded attention when I needed engagement, broken up fights when I needed distraction, and yes, even jumped when I needed amusement.

Is it any wonder that they are my touchstones, my co-therapists, my mantras?

Managing My Anger

MANY PEOPLE NEED to control their anger by learning not to let it out. They can take anger management courses.

My anger problem is I keep it all in. I never know when it's safe to let some of it out. And I don't think they have courses for that.

Why do I need to let my anger out? Wouldn't I be happier and life be easier if I were pleasant and agreeable all the time?

No. There are reasons I need my anger and need to express it.

I need to vent. I was at the office once and a coworker had done some crazy thing or other. I went to my boss and spouted off. Wisely, he just tsk-tsked about it and didn't try to fix anything. He knew that it was just a frustrating situation and I needed to express my feelings.

Stuffing your feelings is unhealthy. It's especially bad if you push the feelings of anger down and then try to smother them with food or alcohol. A character on *Dharma and Greg* once said, "If you're going to bottle up your feelings, you might as well pickle them first." Taking advice from sitcoms is usually not the best idea.

Swallowed feelings don't go away. They stay inside you and fester. Sooner or later you may explode and cause real damage, the kind you can't fix. Better to let off a little anger at times than to save it all for later.

Sometimes, anger is justified. Anger at injustice or when you've been wronged is appropriate. If you don't express it, the injustice or wrongful behavior will simply continue.

Having bipolar disorder makes dealing with my feelings of anger even trickier. I've spent too many years not recognizing that I even have anger and that it's sometimes an appropriate feeling. That leads to becoming a doormat, which I also have years of experience with.

Dealing with my bipolar issues has meant dealing with anger as well. Here are a few things I've learned.

There are people I can vent to. One of them is my therapist; some of my friends provide good outlets too. These are not people I am angry at, at least not when I vent. As with my former boss, I just need someone to hear and acknowledge my feelings of anger. I have separate categories – a friend to discuss my husband with, another one for work issues, and so forth. No one has to listen to too much of my anger spillover.

I need to pick my battles. Living with anyone causes friction, which can lead to anger. Just this week I was mad at my husband. I wanted to shout at him, "If you had done your errands yesterday instead of watching movies, you wouldn't be jammed up today and laying them off on me!" But really, how would that have helped? Could he go back to yesterday and do the errands himself? Would it have helped to refuse to do the errands and then sulk all day? Was there any real reason I couldn't help? Best to let this one go.

I have to measure my words. Perhaps I do this too much, but some amount is necessary. What was helpful this week was to say to my husband, "I need to tell you that I'm frustrated that you left all these errands until today and I had to take over some of them. There were other things I needed to be doing today." By that time, I had cooled off enough that "frustrated" was more accurate than "angry," and less likely to trigger a major shouting match.

If I am angry and I do express it, it's survivable. My husband and I have gotten through some very bad spells when both of us have been extremely angry. Some of them have required couples' therapy, while others have been solved through time and negotiation. Other parts of my life have not turned out as well. I had to cut ties with a toxic relative for whom I had an unhealthy level of anger, with no hope of either of us changing. But I survived, and was the better for it, mentally and emotionally. Sometimes that's necessary, for either your own or the other person's mental health and safety.

It helps to have a good emotional vocabulary. Seriously. I don't have to jump straight to anger when something upsets me. Maybe I really am just frustrated. Or disturbed. Or annoyed. Inconvenienced. Irritated. Miffed. Insulted. Disappointed. Cranky. Those feelings are easy to mistake for anger. It may be better for me to step back and ask, "Do I really feel angry?"

It helps to have a repertoire of behaviors. Not all anger has to be dealt with the same way. I could lash out and say something hurtful. But I could also walk away until I calm down or have a good cry. I could say, "I'm too angry to discuss this now." I could release my anger in a physical activity. I could write a "never-send" letter.

But the first step to all of these is recognizing that I do indeed feel anger and have a right to own my anger and express it. Anger may be harmful, but denying it is harmful too.

Self-Care and Sleep

EVERY ARTICLE YOU SEE about self-care for bipolar disorder will tell you to get enough rest and enough sleep.

> *Sleep is that golden chain that ties health and our bodies together.* – Thomas Dekker

But what did Thomas Dekker know? For many of us, proper, beneficial sleeping is easier said than done.

Even with my prescribed Ambien and Ativan, I've done the wide-awake-at-3:00-don't-get-to-sleep-till-5:30 thing. I've experienced the unsettled-from-nightmares-afraid-to-go-to-sleep thing. Also, the just-one-more-chapter thing. But that's my own fault.

Then the next day I have to take a mega-nap, which leads to guess what? More insomnia.

But this coin has another side as well. There are days when all I do is sleep. A full night of at least 10 hours, then a mega-nap, then right back to bed after dinner.

> *I don't think I was awake for much of my childhood. I did a lot of napping. This might have been a defensive measure against encroaching depression.* – Michael Ian Black

I know that part of my problem is my husband's third shift work schedule — and wanting to be awake at least at some of the same times that he is.

Another part of the problem is my medication. If I wake at 8:30 (yeah, I work at home) and take my meds, I'm down for the count again until at least 10:30. Or 11:00. Or even noon. I hope my clients think that I run errands in the morning or work on my projects with chat, IM, and phone turned off so as not to be disturbed.

And then there is my meal schedule, which is just as erratic as my sleep schedule. Most days I try to eat at least one good, full, hearty meal. But after I eat I get postprandial torpor, the technical term for why you fall asleep on Thanksgiving after eating all that turkey. And there goes another nap.

> *The repose of sleep refreshes only the body. It rarely sets the soul at rest. The repose of the night does not belong to us. It is not the possession of our being. Sleep opens within us an inn for phantoms. In the morning we must sweep out the shadows.* – Gaston Bachelard

But recently, it's been the not-able-to-sleep thing. There's a Tarot card that symbolizes the feeling: the 9 of Swords. In the Rider-Waite deck, the image is of a person sitting up in bed, hiding her face, with nine parallel swords floating in the background. I always refer to it as The Dark Night of the Soul.

> *Sleep is when all the unsorted stuff comes flying out as from a dustbin upset in a high wind.* – William Golding

Anyway, a recent event caused me a fair amount of trauma that I had to suppress at the time, and it came out immediately as bloody horrible nightmares the next time I slept. I haven't had any more of those since, but I suspect they're still lurking at the back of my brain.

> *That we are not much sicker and much madder than we are is due exclusively to that most blessed and blessing of all natural graces, sleep.* – Aldous Huxley

I guess what I mean by all this is that sleep as self-care is wonderful, if it cooperates. But there are so many things that can go wrong and screw it all up: grief, guilt, depression, sorrow, anxiety, fear, loneliness, restlessness, obsessive thoughts, worries. It doesn't feel like something that I have much control over.

Stuffing Your Feelings in a Box

WE ALL KNOW it's a bad idea to stuff your feelings, especially if you then pile food or alcohol on top of them.

The thing is, sometimes you need to suppress a feeling, for just a little while, in order to get through a difficult situation. When that happens, I put my feelings in a box.

Here's an example. My father had only days to live. We all knew it. My mother, who didn't drive, asked me to take her shopping for something to wear at his funeral.

"Do you mind if I don't wear black?" she asked.

"If you don't mind that I do," I replied.

It was my first encounter with a close family death, and I had to get through this awful, wrenching shopping trip. I had to keep my composure so that my mother could keep her composure. I had to steer her away from a flowered dress, which would have been fine for church, to a navy suit and a lighter blue top, which would be suitable for a funeral but not so somber that she couldn't wear it for anything else. All while my father lay in the hospital, dying painfully of bone cancer.

My feelings were complicated, and I absolutely could not afford to feel them at that time. I had to stuff them in a box and close the lid on them until my mother's needs had been met. Then I could let them out, in a time and place where it was safe to, in the presence of a person I could trust with those feelings.

When such circumstances arise, and they will in one form or another, I recommend using a box, one in which the feelings will be out of sight for a while. The box is small; only a few feelings will fit in it. If you think the feelings are going to leak out, you can sit on the lid. Then, when it has served its purpose, you can rip the box open and *feel the feelings*. Cry. Rage. Grieve. That's the important part.

You must experience the grief or fear or even the crushing weight of guilt in order to come through it and heal.

But why put feelings in a box instead of something stronger? Who wants to feel those negative emotions anyway? Aren't we better off without them? Shouldn't you just build a wall around them to keep them from breaking out?

We've all tried it. It works for a while. But a couple of consequences go with the practice. First, *all* your feelings get trapped behind that wall, the good as well as the bad. When you find yourself disconnected from all your feelings, life is a gray blur. In your depression or anxiety or fear or rage, you may not have had many good feelings. But when you build that wall, you cut off even the possibility of having them.

Second, you're only postponing the pain. The wall will leak sometimes. Your unpleasant feelings will come out some way, in your dreams, around your eyes, in sudden spurts, or trickling back into your everyday life. Worse, the wall may shatter, fail altogether, releasing all those feelings in an unstoppable torrent, only stronger and more concentrated from having been confined. They overwhelm both you and anyone in the vicinity. It's not pretty. And it's destructive, to you, your mental health, your healing, your employment, your relationships, to every aspect of your life.

If feelings are behind a wall, you may be able to tell yourself they don't exist. But if you stuff them in a handy box, you can choose the time and place to open it – and yourself – back up.

The Seven Wonders of the Bipolar World

I wonder if I can get out of bed today.
I wonder if a different drug would help.
I wonder what would happen if I told my friends and co-workers.
I wonder how long this mood swing will last.
I wonder if I have enough energy for all I need to do today.
I wonder if people can tell that I have a mental disorder.
I wonder if this is the best I will ever get for the rest of my life.

Chapter 3: The Med-Go-Round

Crazy Pills • Saving Face, or You Can Die From That? • How Psychotropics Helped Me Get My Brain Back • The Overwhelming Problem • Trial and Error • Music Charms the Troubled Mind • Things That Work – Sometimes • Does "Natural" Treatment Work for Depression? • Am I Ready to Stop Therapy? • Running Out of Drugs

Crazy Pills

ONCE UPON A TIME in the land of Jublia lived a kind and powerful queen named Lunesta. One day the dragon Cialis and the evil sorceress Humira attacked the castle, but Jublia was saved by Lunesta and her faithful dog Boniva.

And the peasants rejoiced.

Honestly! The names that pharmaceutical companies give their drugs these days! It's bad enough that the drugs have a list of side effects longer than the symptoms they're supposed to cure. Not to mention the drugs where the side effects *are* the same symptoms they are supposed to cure, or the ones where the side effects are considerably worse than the condition they're being prescribed for.

My favorite has always been, "may cause death" (excuse me, "increases risk of death"). That has to be the ultimate side effect. You'll be dead, but your toenails will look great for the funeral. Leave instructions that include sandals.

I made a list of all the drugs that I've been prescribed in my pursuit of something resembling sanity. It's quite long. I've tried almost every class of drugs there is - tricyclics, atypical, SSRIs, anti-anxiety drugs, and hypnotics - in various combinations and assorted doses, and even for off-label uses. (Did you know that Abilify can be classed as an "atypical atypical," which makes me feel a certain kinship with it?)

The only ones I know I haven't taken are lithium and the MAOI inhibitors. which is a good thing, because I do so like red wine and cheese.

Here's the list, as nearly as I can remember:
Abilify
Buproprion

Desyrel
Effexor
Inderal
Lamictal
Lexapro
Desipramine
Prozac
Sinequan
Tofranil
Topamax
Wellbutrin
Zoloft
Ativan
BuSpar
Ambien
Valium

I may have missed a few, what with the brand names and generics, the decades over which all this occurred, the memory deficits, and the ones I took for only a month or two before the side effects became too heinous.

The side effects I've encountered along the way include:
dry mouth
memory loss
nightmares
agitation
lethargy
weight gain

Not all at the same time, of course, thank heavens. Right now, I seem to have dry mouth, residual memory loss, and weight gain. Given the alternatives, I can live with these. I have to. The memories, I understand, are not coming back. I just hope I don't lose any more, especially the hot-n-juicy variety.

The side effects I haven't suffered include: death (obviously)
fatal skin rash (Stevens-Johnson Syndrome)
tardive dyskinesia

I hope the drug regimen has settled down for a while. I must admit that I don't follow the instructions to the letter. They're simply too overwhelming: Take this one on a full stomach, this on an empty stomach, another with milk, never with grapefruit juice. Something else at bedtime, or half an hour before bedtime, or with the noon meal. And don't forget the non-psychotropics (cholesterol, blood pressure, etc.), or the vitamin, fiber, and calcium my doctor prescribes or recommends. Well, and the OTC Benadryl, Tylenol, and Imodium, as needed.

I did once look up all my meds in a drug interaction database. Every one interacts with every other one. Maybe that's one reason mixing an effective cocktail has been such a crapshoot.

I knew a woman who took so many different drugs for her variety of illnesses and conditions that she had a kitchen timer that she continually set and reset every time she had to take a dose of something. Her meds were more precise than mine, though. If she screwed it up, the consequences would be dire. Her side effects did include death.

The regimen I've settled on is this: one set of pills when I wake up, whenever that is, and one set at 11:00 p.m. I eat whenever I'm hungry, and I don't like grapefruit juice anyway. Anything more complicated than that I can't be sure of remembering. It's still complex, what with the only-in-the-morning pills, the only-at-night pills, and the take-twice-a-day things.

I have little tricks to help me remember the routine: daytime-only pills in a plastic bag, nighttime-only on the lamp base, twice a day on the tea cart. Turn the vitamin bottle upside down after taking morning pills and right-side-up after the evening ones. I suppose I should get one of those daily pill caddy things, but they never seem to have enough, or big enough, compartments.

Is this routine crazy? You should see me without the pills.

Well, no, you shouldn't.

Saving Face, or You Can Die From That?

ONCE, WHEN MY psychiatrist was changing my medication, he warned me about the possible side effects. I know that doctors don't often do this, because they're afraid that the patient will imagine that all the side effects have indeed appeared. So, when he *wanted* to talk about side effects, I perked up my little ears and listened.

"If you notice a rash starting, stop the drug immediately," Dr. R. said. "It could be fatal."

I had never heard of a fatal skin rash before. I had no idea that a skin rash *could* be fatal.

"Don't look at pictures on the Internet," he said. "It's really gross."

Terrific. I might be getting a really gross, possibly fatal skin rash. I probably should have asked for an increased dosage on the anxiety meds.

Of course, I looked it up as soon as I got home. The condition is called Stevens-Johnson Syndrome and apparently the rash is just the beginning. It's possible for your skin to fall off, starting with your face. That's probably the fatal part, as I imagine you'd be prone to infections, plus your insides would now be your outsides. And yes, that would be really gross.

I enlisted my husband's help. "If you notice my skin starting to shred or see a big piece of it lying on the floor, do let me know," I requested. "Maybe pick it up and save it."

Then we debated the merits of duct tape vs. Gorilla Glue for reattaching it.

That was a few years ago. I am still taking the medication and I still have an adequate supply of skin. Now there are commercials on TV for various drugs that list the side effects. I always get a little nostalgic when they list "fatal skin rash" among the possibilities. And just a teensy bit smug because I know what they mean.

The commercials could be fatal too, though. I might die laughing if the next ad was one for Gorilla Glue.

How Psychotropics Helped Me Get My Brain Back

ONE OF THE most difficult challenges for both my doctor and me has been finding the right mix of drugs to get, and keep, me functional at least at some sort of reasonable level. Time to climb on the med-go-round.

While supposedly unipolar, I had been through most of the different sorts of antidepressants and anti-anxiety meds, including, of course, Prozac. When the increasing side effects of each outweighed the diminishing relief, I went through a lengthening list of tricyclics, SSRIs, and so forth. I learned not to ask, "How do they work?" I couldn't get an answer. The more basic question was, "*Do* they work?"

I can't remember all the combinations now. My memory has become Swiss cheese after the spectrum of chemicals I tried. No MAOIs or lithium, though. Those are the big guns of the pharmacopoeia, and I managed to avoid them.

What I do remember all too well is when my brain broke. I don't know what else to call it: nervous breakdown, decompensating, mental and emotional collapse. It wasn't the first time this had happened, I later realized, but it was by far the most severe. And it plunged me deeper into the world of psychotropic drugs.

Each new pill or combo promised (or at least proffered) "Better Living Through Chemistry." I couldn't handle the side effects of some. Others had side effects that I could live with, but little or no therapeutic effect. "There's another drug I'd like to try" was my psychiatrist's constant refrain. That and, "No, we don't know how it works."

We kept going around and around for literally years. With each new med, I had six weeks or so of slowly sliding back into the numbness and misery as my body sloughed off that chemical. Then six or so more weeks, waiting for the new one to work or not, prove tolerable or not, be any better than the previous drug or not. Each new drug cycle amounted to a minimum of three months of hell. More, sometimes, as the doctor slowly, cautiously ramped up the dosage to gauge the effects, both intended and incidental. Lather, rinse, repeat.

Those years are mostly a blur to me now. I couldn't work, and filed for disability, but didn't get it. I wasn't what you'd call able, though. I remember sleeping a lot. I recall not having the wherewithal to add water and nuke a cup of macaroni and cheese. Not bathing. Not feeding the pets. Not paying bills. Not reading. Not caring.

I know now how lucky I was to have a husband who lived the vow about "in sickness and in health" and took up the enormous quantity of slack required. He put up with a distant, unresponsive wife; frequent and apparently unprovoked bouts of sobbing; irrational panics; and all the other symptoms he knew by then he couldn't fix. He didn't know about the suicidal thoughts, or if he suspected, he never mentioned it. He often asked how he could help, but there was nothing else he could do.

Then came the day that my psychiatrist said we were just about out of options. He was thinking of recommending electroshock or ECT, electroconvulsive therapy, its current version. As he talked about how it wasn't like the bad old days and really showed quite good results in some people, his voice seemed to fade, and I heard my inner voice screaming, "Fuck, NO! Keep away from my brain, you Nazi sadist!"

I had heard how in the 1950s electroshock was used as a way to punish or control unruly, uncooperative, or nonconforming women. And of course, most people associate the technique with *One Flew Over the Cuckoo's Nest* and *The Snake Pit*. As far as I was concerned, electroshock was right up (or down) there with icepick lobotomy, the frighteningly efficient nadir of former psychiatric treatments.

Reeling, I made it to my car and immediately called a friend, a scientist, one of the most rational people I know, to talk me down. Her extremely sensible advice was to do some research. Research was something I knew about and vaguely remembered how to do. You could say that the threat of electroshock galvanized me into at least a little effort.

I started digging. Social media was little help. The opinions and experiences of people who had undergone electroshock ranged from "It was hideous" to "It was a miracle." I kept looking and questioning and slogging through the research, as well as the dense fog around me. I lost one friend, my long-time go-to guy for comparing our mental conditions and our meds, who said, "Do it immediately or I will kick your ass."

So, there I was. The pharmaceutical round-about was jolted to a sickening stop by the notion of electrical jolts surging through my brain. What was I doing, considering altering that unique organ with electricity? But the brain in question kept pondering.

Electroshock caused memory lapses. I was already having those.

I would be allowing doctors to tinker with and alter the functioning – perhaps even the structure – of my brain. But really, hadn't I been doing those very things for years with chemicals?

I went back to my psychiatrist, ready to tell him I was at least willing to talk to the doctor who did the shocking.

Then I got a surprise.

"There's one more drug I'd like to try," he said. "Lamictal. It's an anti-seizure drug."

"I don't have seizures. How does it work?"

"We don't really know."

The potential side effects this time were truly daunting. They included depression, memory loss, and a fatal skin rash.

Oh, why the hell not try it? I thought.

So I did. Once more with feelings. More misery. More weeks of weaning off and ramping up. More weeks of no change. The same-old, same-old. Then one day I was in my husband's study and we were talking, when I felt it.

"Oh!" I said. "I remember this. This is the way my brain is supposed to work."

Since then it has kept working, not continuously in the proper manner, but often enough and well enough that I consider the drug a success.

I still had a long way to go, rebuilding the parts of me that I still could and still wanted to. Setbacks. More fiddling with the dosages. The creation of a crazy cocktail of drugs to keep the crazy at bay. And lots and lots of psychotherapy. I was on my way back to functioning, with the help of anti-depressant, anti-anxiety, and anti-seizure drugs, plus a sleeping aid and, eventually, Abilify, which gave me back better concentration and more energy as well. I couldn't have written this without it.

Psychotropic drugs get bad press whenever a spree killer proves to have taken one at some time. They probably are over-prescribed, as some say, or (as I believe) their effects are not well monitored by the prescribers. But in the right combination, with the right support, they can be lifesavers. They certainly were for me.

So, what did I learn from the process? Not "There's always hope." I gave up hope lots of times, every time another med didn't work. Not "Desperate times call for desperate measures." I am infinitely glad I did not have electroshock. "It's always darkest before the dawn"? Please. No truly depressed person believes that crap.

The lesson I took was "Stubbornness is a virtue." Stubbornness has saved our marriage countless times. It saved my father's life for five times longer than the doctors gave him. And it saved my sanity.

"Stubbornness is a virtue" is different from "There's always hope." Even when you *do* give up hope, when you *know* it's hopeless, when you realize the ride is grinding to an inevitable halt, you keep pushing. Hopelessly, if you must, but stubbornly. As long as it takes.

The Overwhelming Problem

IT'S BEEN SAID that time is nature's way of keeping one damn thing after another from being every damn thing all at once. I know that taking things one at a time – eating the elephant one bite at a time – is a sound idea.

However, every now and then the damn things gang up on you. The elephant is starting to go bad and you have to eat all you can right away, to use a disgusting metaphor that I will not take any further. You're welcome.

Last month was one of those months. They happen every so often. If they happen very often I tend to get overwhelmed. And when I get overwhelmed for too long, my brain breaks. I have a meltdown, or I decompensate, or whatever the proper psychiatric term is. In practical terms it means that I'm severely depressed and non-functional for longer than usual. Months. Even years.

The things that overwhelm me are quite predictable: financial difficulties, health problems, relationship glitches, and free-floating anxiety of all sorts. I know that these are situations that cause difficulty for everyone, but to a person with bipolar disorder, they can be insurmountable. Especially when they cluster and refuse to go away.

Over the years I have become better at recognizing when I am about to be overwhelmed. I know the symptoms: the whirling thoughts, the jumping-out-of-my-skin feeling, the insomnia, the inability to concentrate, and the feeling that doom or disaster is impending.

There is little I can do to stave off these feelings. But I know I have to. I have to keep functioning at some level to maintain the things that I want to have: productive work, a loving relationship, a nice house, caring friends, and so forth. At the time of my last major breakdown I came uncomfortably close to losing much of that.

I try my usual remedies for anxiety. I distract myself. I color. I watch mindless TV. I play stupid games on the computer. I turn off my phone. But if the anxiety builds up too much, if the feared disaster is real and impending, none of these things works. The anxiety shreds my last nerve, and the depression starts to settle in. I isolate. I stay in bed. One task at a time, I stop being able to function.

I have taken steps that have helped, however. A few years ago, as the stress was building and approaching the overwhelming stage, I asked my psychiatrist if I could have permission to take one more Ativan a day if I needed it.

He agreed.

I have not needed to take the extra pill every day. Sometimes I take one in the mid-afternoon if I start feeling jumpy, twitchy, or panicky. Sometimes I take one at night if I haven't gotten to sleep within 2 - 3 hours after taking my regular nighttime pills. I know it sounds strange that a depressant helps me stave off depression, but my diagnosis is bipolar disorder *and* anxiety disorder. The Ativan catches me at the point where the one starts to turn into the other.

I'm glad my psychiatrist trusted me not to abuse what I consider a privilege as well as a necessity. By the time I made this request, of course, we had been working together for years and had built up a certain trust. I think there have been only a couple of times when I have had to take two extra Ativan in a day, one in the afternoon *and* an additional one at night. And both times, I felt guilty about it and made sure I didn't make it a habit.

I don't want to start gobbling pills at the least sign of difficulty. All I want is to be able to eat my elephant in pieces and in peace.

Trial and Error

I RECENTLY READ an article in *Discover* magazine called "The Power of Single-Person Medical Experiments." The article discussed the fact that the usual clinical studies of new drugs and treatments, randomized, double-blinded, hundreds or thousands of participants, the "gold standard" of tests and trials, give results that are only averages. The techniques will work for some people and not for others. Some experimental subjects will experience side effects to varying degrees. Some won't.

The only way to see whether a given treatment works for an individual is for that person to try it. The odds may say it has a better-than-50-percent chance of working, but until the patient tries it, whether it will work *for that one individual* is basically a roll of the dice.

I think this may be particularly true of psychotropics. Every time I've asked how this or that med works, the answer has been, "We don't really know." Factor in the number of different meds I'm on, psychotropic and otherwise, and their potential for interactions with each other, and any new treatment's effectiveness is likely a matter of trial and error.

I've certainly gone through a long, tedious, disappointing, and unpleasant series of weaning off and ramping up different meds in hopes of mixing just the right cocktail for my particular brain.

I think that's why they call it "practicing" medicine.

Music Charms the Troubled Mind

ONCE I KNEW a man whose wife was going to leave him. I knew he was in a lot of pain and despair about it, though he also turned into a huge asshole before everything was said and done. He was also suicidal for a time.

One day when I was trying to talk him through a bad patch, I asked whether he might turn to music to help him.

"What?" he said. "Do you think I should listen to country music and cry in my beer?"

I wasn't suggesting that at all. I just knew that he was a singer and songwriter of talented amateur status and was known for this in various circles. I honestly thought that music might help.

To be fair, in a downswing I always forget how much music can do for me. It soothes and heals, but it also lets me tap into the emotions that I have been suppressing.

Do I have the inexplicable blues that are part and parcel of my condition? There's a song for that. Am I feeling unrequited love? Unrequited lust? There's a song for those too. Is the world spinning too fast for me? Do I need to know that everything will be all right? Or do I just need to know that someone, somewhere and somewhen, has also felt this way? I can turn to music.

> *Music, uniquely among the arts, is both completely abstract and profoundly emotional. It has no power to represent anything particular or external, but it has a unique power to express inner states or feelings. Music can pierce the heart directly; it needs no mediation."* – Oliver Saks, *Musicophilia*

Saks also says, "The power of music, whether joyous or cathartic, must steal on one unawares, come spontaneously as a blessing or a grace." There he and I part company.

Music can certainly steal on us unawares, whack us upside the head with a memory, a feeling, a piercing stab of emotional intensity, all the stronger for being unexpected. But we can also choose to bring music into our lives when nothing else seems to touch us. We can tap into those memories and feelings, good or bad, and let the music wash over us as we listen and feel.

According to scientific experiments with fMRI,, or functional Magnetic Resonance Imaging, music uses more parts of the brain than almost any other activity. The neural connections fire all over the place, more so if one is playing an instrument, but even when just listening. The memory centers, artistic areas, language centers, emotional areas, and even the motor complexes, are stimulated.

My problem is remembering all that music can do for me. When my emotions are dulled, flattened by the steamroller of depression, I sometimes forget that I can be any other way. The music I love is always there for me. I can bathe in it, wallow in it, be uplifted by it, float on it, join in with it, feel it emotionally, viscerally, and intellectually, individually or all at once. It can express the things that I just can't.

When you're depressed, it's a time for writing bad poetry. Or you can let good poets and songwriters take you with them as they explore the human condition in ways you're not capable of. I think that's why they do it, create their art. The good ones anyway.

There's also something to be said for music as distraction. A song from years ago, even a frivolous one, can take you away from your troubles, even if only for a moment. This is not the time for exploring new musical avenues. Remembering that things once were good can feed your sadness, your depression, but it can also give you perspective. If you took joy in this music once, there will come a time when you will again. And maybe that time is now.

Perhaps the most amazing power of music is to provoke catharsis. Certain songs leave me sobbing like a baby. They don't even have to be sad songs, though many of them are. "The Mary Ellen Carter" by Stan Rogers is about as life-affirming as you can get, but it can still turn me into a weeping puddle. His song "Lies" has nothing to do with my situation personally, but its evocative power touches me nonetheless. And almost no one I know can make it through Kathy Mar's "Velveteen."

Afterwards, I feel drained and, if not exactly better, less emotionally constipated, I guess you'd say. Clearing away a bit of blockage can be cleansing. If music can do that then I don't care if it's country with a beer, jazz with a glass of wine, or hip hop with an energy drink. Even easy listening with a glass of milk, if that's your thing.

Thank God and Apple for iTunes. And here's hoping that my Swiss cheese of a memory will give me a nudge in the right direction when I need it next time.

Things That Work – Sometimes

RIGHT NOW, I am in the middle of a fairly deep depression. It has gone on for days, which is unusual now that I am more or less stabilized on medication. But there is no let-up in sight.

This time it's one of those I-have-nothing-to-look-forward-to moments, plus the holidays, plus the need-to-see-my-therapist thing, plus the have-an-appointment-with-new psychiatrist-but-it's-not-for-five-months thing, plus the whole no-spoons-to-get-out-but-really-need to-get-out-of-the-house feeling, plus the various catastrophizing-about-finances-and-the-IRS problems, plus the there's-something-I-really-want-to-happen-but-if-it-does-it-won't-be-soon-and-may-not-happen-at-all.

Let's see. Is there anything else?

Oh, probably, but that will do for starters. Of course, to a lot of people, those would be everyday annoyances and I would be having your standard pity party. But for a bipolar person, with my brain chemistry, it's an invitation to a deep, dark pit.

What are the things that help pull me through, or out, or up? And what are the things I can do while I just ride it out?

Well, there's music. There are two long-form musical bits that have been known to lure me out: *The Mikado* and *The Pirates of Penzance*. Occasionally when I haven't gotten out of bed in a while, my husband will put on a DVD of one or the other and wait for me to appear in the door of his study. There is usually beer or snacks, and I can sing along, badly but loudly, to my heart's content. Heart's content, now there's a good thing. Going to see live productions of Gilbert & Sullivan was an activity my sorority used to do, and one of my best memories of otherwise-difficult sorority life.

Then there are distractions. These don't actually improve my mood, but they can help me avoid dwelling on the above list of what's-wrongs. If I have the concentration needed to read, that's my go-to choice. I usually try to keep one fiction and one nonfiction going, so I can switch back and forth.

Sometimes, though, I don't have the concentration to make it through a chapter. Then it's time to try TV. Something familiar, non-challenging, not too fast-paced. Cooking shows work, or something like *Pawn Stars*. True crime or true medicine. Shows where I already know the characters and the back-stories: *Castle, Bones*.

When I don't even have enough concentration for that, I go for stupid games. One or two rounds of Bingo Blitz are about as mindless as you can get and still be breathing. Or I can turn off my brain entirely, play obsessively, and get lost for hours of not-worrying about anything more important than filling out a straight in the gin rummy program on my tablet.

Occasionally I can do light-as-popcorn forms of social interaction. Phone calls with a depressed friend or one who always has a silly joke ready or one who reads the same sorts of things that I do. Instant messaging. Facebook lurking.

Sometimes, though not often in this state, I can force myself to work a little. Or work on my blogs. It's difficult and not really satisfying and sometimes even painful, but if I can do it, it's probably the best thing for me. Accomplishing something, anything, helps build a step out of the pit.

As for the usual advice, rest, exercise, nutrition, meditation, I usually can't manage those. Except for sleeping. I'm a world-class napper. Also, a world-class insomniac. Don't ask me how I manage that. It's a gift. My husband makes sure I eat at least one good meal a day. For meditation I pet a cat. I still haven't gotten the exercise thing worked out yet.

Then I wait.

I know that the depression will not last for weeks or months or years the way it used to. I'm just going to be miserable until I'm not anymore.

Does "Natural" Treatment Work for Depression?

NOT FOR EVERYONE, and not all of the time.

Angel Chang recently posted on LittleThings.com "The 10 best natural ways to treat depression." While she does acknowledge that "clinical depression is triggered from within, and very often need[s] medical attention" and "it's imperative to consult your physician if you notice an abrupt change in your mood, feelings, or sense of well-being," her article is about "easy" ways to treat depression yourself.

Unfortunately, her tips are not very helpful for me and many others who suffer from clinical bipolar or unipolar depression. Here's how I respond to them.

Meditate. This is both nearly impossible when you have racing thoughts, and a way to sink even lower if you can't clear your mind of negative thoughts, which is one of the hallmarks of depression. If you're manic, even sitting still in one place for any length of time can be a challenge. After you're stabilized on medication, go for it.

Eat Foods with Vitamin B. It may be true that vitamin B has been linked to neurotransmitters that we need more of, but preparing food is not very likely when I'm in the Pit of Despair. I try to imagine myself preparing a meal of fish, Swiss cheese, spinach, and eggs, and I just can't. Or shopping for them. I might be able to scramble an egg in the microwave, but that's about it. I do take a multivitamin along with my bedtime psychotropics, so I guess I can follow this advice a bit.

Set goals. Chang recommends starting with "small, daily goals." When in full-blown depression, mine are about as small as you can get. Get out of bed. Make it through the day without crying. Take my meds. Poof! Out of spoons! Chang quotes an expert who gives an example of a goal to work up to as washing the dishes every other day. To me, that implies a series of goals: Gather up dishes. Find soap. Fill sink. Wash a dish. Put in drainer. Repeat. My tip: wash the spoons first!

Sleep on a schedule. Going to bed at the same time every night may be do-able but getting up at the same time isn't possible for me, which is one of the reasons I can't hold a regular job. An alarm clock awakening me before my body is ready leaves me groggy and unfit to work. And there's no guarantee that I'll sleep during those scheduled hours, even with Ambien. Chang advises not taking naps, but I seldom make it through the day without one, even if I have slept eight or nine or ten hours. In fact, I love naps and consider them therapeutic, for me at least. Naps are my friends.

Get out of your rut. Structure is the only thing that keeps some of us going. And if we could find joy in a painting class, a museum, or making a new friend, as Chang suggests, we probably wouldn't be depressed in the first place. J. K. Rowling described the Dementors in the Harry Potter books: "Get too near a Dementor and every good feeling, every happy memory will be sucked out of you. ... You will be left with nothing but the worst experiences of your life." She has stated that they are metaphors for depression. With every good feeling sucked out of you, you can't see anything but the rut. I am told that for some people, Cognitive Behavioral Therapy (CBT) lessens the tendency to keep traveling in the rut. But "easy" and "natural"? I don't know.

Talk. Chang is advocating talking with trusted loved ones, which is good as far as it goes. What it ignores is that friends and loved ones are not universally understanding of depression or supportive in dealing with it. She never suggests talking with a therapist or doctor. I don't know why that's less "natural" than talking with someone who has no training. Except you have to pay them, but painting or language classes or art supplies aren't free either.

Exercise. This is a classic antidote for depression, and I understand that it works for many people some of the time. But I would put this under the same heading as setting goals. I know it would be good for me, but motivation is hard to come by and immobilization thwarts me. But I wish I could take this advice. I investigated water aerobics, but there's not a feasible program in my area.

Responsibilities. "Because you might feel down," the article states, "you may also want to withdraw from your daily activities in life and your responsibilities at home or at work." Yeppers. "Try staying involved as much as possible in the causes you care deeply about and take on new daily responsibilities. These can be as simple as volunteering at your local food pantry or going back to work part-time." Big nope. See getting out of your rut, above. For many of the clinically depressed, working even part-time is unimaginable, with responsibilities of the crushing sort.

Unwind and relax. If your depression comes with anxiety like mine, this idea is a non-starter. Unless you count drinking as relaxation, though it isn't the best idea if you're on meds.

Stay off caffeine. Okay, I can pretty much do this one, except for one cup of coffee or a caffeinated soda to get me started in the morning.

"Did you learn something new about how to naturally treat symptoms of depression?" the article ends. Not really. Well, except for the B vitamins. We've all heard these kinds of advice before. They're good tips for situational or reactive depression, but largely not feasible for the chronically, clinically, biochemically depressed. In a way they add up to the much-hated "Just stop it. You must want to be depressed or else you'd be doing all these great things."

But try them if you can, perhaps in addition to medical treatments. Maybe some of the ones that won't work for me will for you. In the meantime, get help. See your therapist and/or psychiatrist. Keep taking those meds. Those may not be "easy, natural" ways to treat depression, but if they work, isn't that the larger point?

P.S. Do NOT Google "CBT." Spell out "Cognitive Behavioral Therapy." Trust me on this one.

Support and Non-Support

MY FAMILY HAS never been big on support groups. When my father had multiple myeloma, which killed him after 15 years, he turned down any opportunities he was given to join cancer support groups with names like Make Today Count. He preferred to go it alone. He was stubborn. So am I.

I have been to support groups for mental illness once or twice, but they were never a success or, I guess, just never right for me.

The first one was when I was in college. That one was a bust because I wasn't ready to address my problems and because I had the ability to appear "normal" for an hour at a time while sitting cross-legged on the floor. I couldn't do the floor-sitting part now.

The second time was after I saw a brochure for a group called High Flyers and Low Landers, which met in the church I was going to at the time.

It was a very odd experience. Everyone had a book, many with needlepoint covers. It was their bible, though not *the* Bible, which I know many people needlepoint covers for, or at least did back then.

The meetings consisted of a little ritual. One person read a passage from the book. Then each person in the circle had to tell an event that happened to him or her in the past week. The recital had to be in a specific format: what happened, what symptoms the person experienced, dry mouth, racing thoughts, and so on down the list, how the person would have handled it before reading the book, and how the person did handle it. There was much quoting of the book and certain specific phrases that everyone had to use.

Some of the quotations were helpful, or at least true, such as, people do things *that* annoy us, not *to* annoy us. But as I recall, those were the only sorts of comments the people in the circle were allowed to make. Not "How did that work out?" or "What did your mother do next?" or "I hate when people get passive-aggressive."

As I was leaving, I offered someone a mint. Everyone laughed and said, "Dry mouth!" It was just too weird and formulaic for me, so I never went back. Since I don't seem to do so well in physical support groups, I recently thought I would check out some virtual ones. I'm not going to name the groups I joined or where I found them, because all of them stressed privacy and confidentiality.

What I found was both support and non-support.

Some of the groups were associated with national organizations or publications, and they pretty much stuck to sharing articles about scientific research or political news about mental illness, along with lists of resources, hotlines, and the like.

So far, so good.

Other groups were more like traditional support groups, with members asking questions or relating accounts of what had happened or how they felt. There were administrators who encouraged the members to more or less stick to the topic and rules of the group: give trigger warnings, no suicide threats, or whatever.

Some of the groups were peaceful. People asked standard questions. Who's on this med? Should I take something else too? They received fairly standard answers. Worked for me. Didn't work for me. Ask your doctor. People related similar events and how they handled them or asked for more specifics so they could understand the situation better. People posted assorted uplifting memes and affirmations.

Then there was the other sort. People did not know how to use trigger warnings or simply didn't bother. Others shared people's posts without removing identifying information. Some posted truly vulgar jokes that had nothing whatsoever to do with bipolar disorder. Negativity overflowed. Arguments raged. Some of the topics were "Bipolar is not an excuse for bad behavior" and "Don't buy into the drug companies' propaganda by taking meds." There was the online equivalent of name-calling and shouting. People reported other people to the admins. People accused people of reporting people to the admins.

The administrators did try to keep a handle on these groups, but couldn't always, most likely because they were busy with their own lives and issues and difficulties.

It got so bad that I took to lurking instead of participating. Every week or so I would go back to take a peek and check on the drama llamas. Mostly they were still running around spitting. I think I had helpful things to add to the discussions and times when I needed help with feelings, but I just couldn't trust enough to jump back in. I know other people left these groups for similar reasons, and some were blocked or banned or given warnings about their behavior.

In general, I have this to say about online support groups. You'd do well to sit back and watch their interactions before you try participating on anything but a "Congratulations! You got a job!" level. If the group seems truly helpful and supportive then dive in. You may be able to give and receive help.

But non-support is exhausting. And I'm too stubborn to put up with it.

Am I Ready to Stop Therapy?

I GOT MY first hint that I might be ready to stop therapy when I realized how little I was going. Over the years I've scaled down from weekly sessions to biweekly.

Then I noticed that, effectively, I've been going only once a month. I've been forgetting appointments, showing up on the wrong day, oversleeping, feeling poorly physically, or having too much freelance work to do.

Of course, those could be signs that I'm in denial, that I'm resisting therapy, that we've hit a bad patch of difficult issues and I just don't want to deal with them.

But I don't think that's what's happening. Here's why.

I'm stabilized on my medications and they're effective. When my psychiatrist moved away a few months ago, he left me with enough refills to last until this month and a list of other psychiatrists. My PCP agreed to prescribe my psychotropics if I lined up another psychiatrist for emergencies. I did that, though I couldn't get an appointment until months later.

And that didn't alarm me. I don't have the oh-my-god-what-if-my-brain-breaks-again panics. I don't have the feeling that my brain *is* about to break again. I've thought about it, and I'm comfortable with letting my involvement with the psychiatric profession fade into the background of my life.

As long as I keep getting my meds.

I have more good days and I'm beginning to trust them. Oh, I still question whether I'm genuinely feeling good, happy, and productive or whether I'm merely riding the slight high of hypomania. But really? It doesn't seem to matter very much. A few days ago, I reflected on a string of particularly good days when I accomplished things, enjoyed my hobbies, and generally felt content. And I simply allowed myself to bask in those feelings.

That's not to say I don't still have bad days. After a few days of hypomania, I hit the wall, look around for spoons, don't find any, and require mega-naps to restore me. I'm intensely grateful that I work at home and can do that. Most offices don't appreciate finding an employee snoring underneath her desk. And my cat-filled bed is much comfier-cozier.

I still get low days too, but they are noticeably dysthymic rather than full-out, sobbing-for-no-reason, Pit-of-Despair-type lows that last seemingly forever. I know, really *know*, deep within me, that they will last a day or two at the most. And just that knowledge makes me feel a little bit better.

My creativity, concentration, and output are improving. I can work longer, read longer, write longer, take on new projects, think past today or even next week. I can trust my muse and my energy, if not immediately when I call on them, at least within a reasonable time.

I have trouble remembering how bad it used to be. Recently I've made connections with several on-line support groups for bipolar and mental health. I find I'm astonished at the crises, the outpourings of misery, the questioning of every feeling and circumstance, the desperate drama of even the most mundane interactions. They are overwhelming. But I realized that it's been a long time since they've overwhelmed *me*. I recognize that I could someday be in that place again. That's the nature of this illness. But I have a good support system that I trust to help me not fall too far without a net.

I don't have much to talk about when I go to therapy. There are issues I need to work on – getting older, getting out of the house more, reclaiming my sexuality. But most of those I feel competent to work out on my own. My sessions are mostly an update on what's going on in my life at the moment, plus a recap of my recurring problems. But those problems are ones I've faced before and know how to cope with. I already have the tools I need and use them without needing a reminder.

I've talked it over with my psychotherapist and while I'm not completely quitting therapy, but I am cutting back officially to the once a month I seem to be going anyway. I know that if and when the bipolar starts giving me major trouble again, I can always call for an appointment or a telephone session.

Running Out of Drugs

RUNNING OUT OF your medications is scary.

I know. It's happened to me several times in the last few months.

Sometimes it was a matter of supply. My usual pharmacy ran out of Ambien and wasn't going to get any more until after the weekend. Fortunately, they recommended a mom-and-pop pharmacy just down the street and helped me transfer my prescription there.

Another time the problem was the prescription. I ran out of Ativan, but when I called in for a refill, I was told that it wasn't time for one. When I looked at the bottle more closely, I discovered that they had given me 60 pills, as if I were taking two a day, instead of the three a day prescribed. I was changing doctors about that time and there was miscommunication.

Yet another time, it was money. I ran out of Abilify and was told that even with insurance, it would cost me $800 because of the out-of-pocket required minimum. I spent a couple of days arguing with the insurance company, researching solutions online, and making sure a local pharmacy would take the coupon I found, which lowered the price to under $200.

And, of course, there are the everyday screw-ups. My husband forgot to pick up my scrips, or forgot which pharmacy they were at, or didn't hear me say that I was completely out, or the pharmacy didn't open until 10:00, or they had my pills in two different bags and only gave us one. There are lots of ways it can happen.

Once I even took my entire supply on a weekend getaway and left them in a drawer in the bed-and-breakfast. I know. Stupid.

Most of the time running out of drugs isn't a crisis. It just feels like one.

Of course, there are exceptions. It *is* a crisis if you run out of certain anti-anxiety drugs and you don't get any for several days. You can have physical and psychological withdrawal. I've heard that benzo withdrawal can be as bad as withdrawal from opiates. That's one reason it's important to replace your meds as soon as possible.

A lot of psychotropic medications build up to a therapeutic level in your bloodstream, so a day or two without them probably won't even be noticeable. When you start taking them again, your levels will even out.

But even if the med you run out of is one that you can easily tolerate a day or two without, you may have psychological effects. When I run out of a prescription, even for a short time, I become twitchy and agitated, my hypomania kicks in, coming out as anxiety like usual. I fear crashing back into that deadly unmedicated space where all is misery and despair. Intellectually, I know that likely won't happen. But it sure *feels* like it will. This is one way my none-too-stable mind plays tricks on me.

It's like the opposite of the placebo effect, believing that a medication will help you and experiencing gains even if the pill is fake. In this version, I believe that *not* taking the pill will cause relapse, even though it won't.

Whatever else you feel or do, DO NOT use missing a couple of pills as an opportunity to go off your meds entirely. This is a lie your brain can tell you: "You're doing fine without it. Why keep taking it?" It may not be right away, but you *will* feel the effects of not taking your meds, and then there you are, back in the Pit of Despair or rocketing to the skies. It won't be pretty.

For me and a lot of others like me, the key to effective medication is consistency. Once you find the right "cocktail," stick with it. But if you run out, don't panic. Keep Calm & Get a Refill.

Chapter Four: Family Matters

Bipolars, Rollercoasters, and Sex • A Portrait of the Blogger as a Young Bipolar • A Bipolar Child • A Grain of Salt • Mini-Meltdowns and Many Meltdowns • Family Matters • A Mother? Me? • Mr. Fix-It • Taking Turns • How a Cat Helped Me Stay Sane

Bipolars, Rollercoasters, and Sex

THE ROLLERCOASTER is the most common metaphor for bipolar disorder. But is it really the best one?

After all, a rollercoaster has long, abrupt downward swoops, and anticipatory highs. But rollercoaster highs crank slowly, grindingly up. Mania isn't like that. Boom! You're suddenly at the top.

Nor are rollercoaster lows like the lows of depression. If they were, the downward slide would not be the exhilarating, thrilling part of the ride, and would not immediately be followed by another high. Instead the rollercoaster would plod along through a lengthy trough, or maybe a tunnel, with no idea of when the next up would come.

Perhaps a seesaw is a better metaphor. Its ups and downs are quick, and you can stay stuck in either position for an undetermined length of time. And a seesaw is all about balance.

But no. A seesaw requires a second person to operate correctly, and that is certainly not the experience of a bipolar person. Our brain chemistry alone is enough to get us going up and down.

A pogo stick? The spring gets squashed and then rebounds. But it's a rhythmic bounce, not one that you don't see coming until you're in it.

The basic problem with most of the usual metaphors is that they involve fun at some level. Bipolar is not fun. Oh, the mania may be enjoyable for a time. But the gut-wrenching drop does not make you go "whee!"

So how about a soufflé? It can rise or fall, and you never quite know which it's going to do.

Or a computer? It can open up the world, but is going to crash sometime, inevitably when you most need it to work.

I suppose we could split it up. Mania is a fountain and depression is a ditch. Depression is a b&w rabbit-ear TV and mania is cable with 1000 channels. Mania is a battery and depression is a dead battery.

The root of the problem is that no metaphor can adequately explain bipolar disorder. Even Spoon Theory, useful as it is, explains only the effects, not how the disorder itself works and feels. A metaphor may capture one half of the experience, the ups or the downs, but not the reality of both.

If it's not possible to explain bipolar disorder with a metaphor, why do we so often try to? Because, really, only people with bipolar know what it is like, and the experience even differs from person to person. A psychologist or psychiatrist may understand the mechanisms and the biochemistry and the complications and the medications. But she or he is essentially watching from the outside.

My husband didn't really "get" depression until he fell into depression himself that lasted a couple of weeks.

"Now," I said, "try to imagine that feeling lasting for months."

He couldn't, but at least he was closer to understanding.

My mother-in-law, who doesn't "believe in" mental illness, now has a clue too, since she experienced a profound reactive depression.

Neither of them really "gets" mania.

Maybe the best metaphor is that bipolar disorder is like sex. You can't adequately explain it to someone who's never had it. And even when you've had either sex or bipolar disorder, you only know what it's like *for you*. You can generalize your experience and share commonalities, but basically, every case of bipolar is something a person goes through alone, or maybe alone together as Jenny Lawson says.

Bipolar disorder.
It is what it is.

A Portrait of the Blogger as a Young Bipolar

I WAS DEPRESSED even as a child. I may have been manicky too, but I don't remember that. Unless you count the anxiety. I had weird fears – for example, that someone might toss a lit cigarette out of a car window just as another car with a leaky gas tank went by and there would be a huge explosion and fire. Stuff like that.

I won't say that bullying caused my mental condition, because I now know that brain chemistry is the more likely culprit. But bullying certainly made it worse.

In addition to the usual taunts about "cooties," my appearance, and my complete cluelessness about social skills, I was singled out because I was smart and liked school and didn't hide it.

As I look back on it, some of the bullying now seems extreme.

There was the boy who chased me around the playground, threatening me with what he claimed was a hypodermic needle.

There were the kids at the bus stop who threw rocks at me while I tried to pretend it was a game of dodge-rock. Never being good at sports, I came out of that episode with three stitches in my forehead. I don't know which upset me more, but by the end of it all, I was hysterical. And not the good, funny kind.

And there was my best friend and the birthday party. The party was for her younger sister and all the attendees were about that same age. My BFF and I were supposed to be supervising, I guess. But while I was blindfolded, demonstrating Pin the Tail on the Donkey, she kicked me in the ass. Literally. In front of all those younger kids.

This resulted in what I now realize was my first breakdown (meltdown, freak-out, whatever you call it). Naturally I ran home sobbing and spent nearly a week curled in a fetal position, alternately crying my eyes out and going numb. I stayed like that until I saw my mother crying. Then I got up, went down the street and yelled at the former BFF for indirectly making my mother cry.

It's a wonder I'm not a spree killer today.

A Bipolar Child

I SUPPOSE I WAS a bipolar child. I don't really know, but I assume I was, because now I'm a bipolar adult.

I think I was more of a depressed child, which makes sense, since I have bipolar 2, with depressive episodes far outnumbering hypomanic ones. There were some times, though, when I would laugh loudly and inappropriately in class, triggered by a word that reminded me of something funny I'd read. There were times I'd walk around with a village-idiot grin because of some minor accomplishment like winning a live goldfish at a school fair.

But mostly I remember misery. Tears. Loneliness. Hysterics. Confusion. Isolation. Hurt. Despair.

I'm fairly sure my depression wasn't mostly reactive, although parts of it surely were. The bullying, betrayals by friends, not understanding social conventions: All these were things that could easily make a person depressed, regardless of brain biochemistry.

But by and large my life was what would be considered pretty damned idyllic. I had stable, loving parents, a comfortable home in the suburbs with good schools, all the food I wanted, and as many toys as I could play with. I had a sister and a neighborhood full of children my age, but I remember being perpetually lonely. I had a good education but looking back I realize that my illness prevented me from getting the most from it. There was no sexual or physical abuse and no neglect. No one close to me died or suffered major trauma, at least until I was in high school and my parents suffered illnesses. Even then, they did a good job of keeping life as normal as possible. At the time we never felt it was a tragedy. It was just something we got through together.

That just leaves endogenous depression, or, at least, the depression half of bipolar disorder. I remember one day walking home from elementary school and thinking, "All these houses look so pretty, but the people in them aren't all happy." It was somewhat of a revelation to me. I had several major meltdowns, and hundreds of smaller depressive episodes. I had nervous twitches and tics and was prescribed Valium for them.

During my high school years, it was suggested that perhaps I ought to go to the school district's psychologist. My parents, who were not really familiar with mental illness and psychiatry, asked me if I wanted to go. I didn't. I probably should have, although back then it's fairly unlikely that I would have been diagnosed with bipolar disorder of any type. I might have gotten some help for the depression, though. They might have taken me off the Valium.

Like most lonely and misunderstood and depressive kids, I found my salvation in books. They were friends, distractions, instruction manuals on how to survive, food for my emptiness, a place to lose myself when the world was too much with me. By and large it worked, at least as well as anything could, a self-prescribed and self-regulated form of instinctual bibliotherapy.

These were not books on how to make friends or teaching a child how to cope with emotions. They were for the most part pure escapism. Fantasy and science fiction, mysteries and adventures, literature and bestsellers. A complete mishmash of classics and trash. Those were my doctors, my therapists, my Prozac, my mood stabilizers.

I look back now on myself as a child, mentally disordered, undiagnosed, untreated, and wonder how I survived as much as I did.

If I were a child these days, would I get the help that I needed then? Would my parents recognize that I was not just odd and unhappy, but mentally ill? Would I have been diagnosed properly? Medicated properly? Counseled properly?

With all that needs to go right and all that can go wrong during the process, it feels like getting help for a bipolar child certainly was, and perhaps still is, pretty much of a crapshoot. I made it through, but I hope it's easier these days for a kid like me.

A Grain of Salt

THIS WEEK HAS been bad. I tried to poke my nose out from under the rock where I've been hiding from the world.

Bad idea. I was instantly overwhelmed by the crazy-stupid-crazy of various sorts that has been sucking up all the oxygen lately. Read James Thurber's story "A Box to Hide In." I was safe in the box and then I tried to come out.

Mistake. The sheer volume of malignant idiocy in the world seemed to have increased exponentially in the intervening week. I tried to stay away from it, refused to dip my smallest nerveless toe into Facebook threads on topics I have strong opinions about. A friend called to see whether I was okay, and I had a mini-meltdown.

I really thought my brain was going to break again.

It wasn't just the relentless assault from the outside, though that was more than plenty.

I also had internal stress. My work. My difficulty forcing myself to do it. My exhaustion once I had done it. My total lack of spoons, even plastic ones.

The friend who called suggested a day off, comfort food, a book, cats. All good suggestions, and I tried them all.

The problem was, when I shut off all that other noise, memories began haunting me. Ones from years ago that I've never been able to suppress completely. From a time in my life when my psychiatric problems were undiagnosed and untreated, my body began to be plagued with conditions I still live with, my self-esteem was nonexistent, and my soul was being sucked dry by a person who might have helped but made all of those things worse.

Today is still rough, but I had one good memory return. My husband bought a watermelon and I sprinkled a piece with salt.

This was a thing that my family used to do in the summertime – sit at the backyard picnic table and eat watermelon lightly sprinkled with salt. And of course, compete to spit seeds the farthest.

The combination of salt and sweet is a trend among foodies these days, with the new sensation, salted caramel. Believe me, we were not foodies. Served with the watermelon were home-made popsicles made from Kool-Aid in Tupperware molds.

But for me, watermelon with just a touch of salt was one of the hallmarks of summer that I have not experienced in years. It was right up there with going barefoot and climbing trees.

My husband tried the melon with salt, but it didn't do the same for him. It's not one of his childhood pleasures, and he hates to add salt to anything, even popcorn. But at least he tried it and listened to my story.

Mostly when a memory leaps suddenly into my mind, it's the haunting kind. But every once in a while I get salted watermelon. And I am grateful.

Mini-Meltdowns and Many Meltdowns

WHEN MY BRIAN BROKE back in 2001 or so, I thought it was the first time that had happened. Later, on reflection, it turned out that wasn't so.

The 21st-century breakdown was certainly the most dramatic. Although I had just quit working in an office to start a freelance career, I found myself unable to work after a few months.

I had become unable to work in the office because of mounting difficulties that I now realize were warning signs of the impending breakdown: inability to concentrate, increased anxiety, the feeling that an angry badger was about to claw its way out of my stomach, lessened ability to interact with coworkers, sudden flares of temper, turning people away with unintentionally cutting remarks and sarcasm, isolating, inappropriate affect, catastrophizing. You name it, I had it.

What was causing all these symptoms? My bipolar disorder, obviously. But I've had that for years. What was pushing me over the edge this time? I had trouble at work. My boss left and, when I "came out" to my new boss as depressed, she reacted with wariness and incomprehension. She gave me the first bad review I ever had at that job.

My mother's health was deteriorating seriously, too, about then. I lost time at work taking her to various appointments and I had to have "the talk" with her about how much longer she could live alone. Eventually I took over her finances but by then was scarcely handling my own.

I experienced a lift when I quit my job and began freelancing. Hypomania? You bet! My new flexibility allowed me to take better care of my mother, and the assignments kept coming in.

Then everything came crashing down. I screwed up my finances and my mother's. She began having worse falls and injuries, hospital stays and drug reactions, even hallucinations which scared the hell out of me. I emotionally judo-ed my sister to come up and help, then fought with and resented her, and had to take care of parts of her life as well.

Those and other difficulties on top of my mental disorder added up to a non-functioning me. I dumped all the chores and coping onto my husband, which was a rotten thing to do. I fought with him, sobbed for no discernible reason, became unable to work, or care, or do much of anything except think up at least three different reasons and ways to kill myself. Fortunately, I was too immobilized to try any of them.

I've written before about the things that helped me get back to some kind of functioning, a proper diagnosis, the right meds, time without work, lots of psychotherapy, and my wonderful, patient, ever-helpful, devoted husband. But now, looking back, I can see that it had happened before, though not so dramatically and completely. In childhood, in my teens, in college, at every stage of my life I had at least one breakdown, often triggered by the circumstances of my life, but fueled and stoked by my mental illness. In every one my ability to function deteriorated a little more.

I had a mini-meltdown in my freshman year of college, which involved sitting in my nightgown in the hallway, staring for hours at a richly detailed poster of a fantasy realm. I managed to frighten an intruder by arising, ghost-like, in my pale-yellow shroud of a nightgown as he entered the suite.

This one was triggered by my realization that I had probably chosen the wrong major and that there were no job prospects ahead for me. It turns out I was wrong about that. Maybe I should have stuck with it, but my next choice turned out pretty well. I took a year off college and a job as a cashier in a restaurant, where I spent a lot of time crying into the roller towel and being told I should smile more. This convinced me that going back to college, with a new major, was the right thing to do, even if there were fewer job prospects.

The next meltdown was major. I had finished college, endured a year-long train wreck of a relationship, and lost a job as an assistant restaurant manager. I got unemployment, which meant I lay around the apartment for most of the week, except for the half-hearted attempts at job hunting.

One notable symptom of this breakdown was my near-complete immobility. One errand in a day, say, going to the post office for stamps, made it a productive one for me. I had maybe three of those a month, with one being the obligatory visit to the unemployment office, a supremely depressing place to be depressed.

I had some truly irrational thinking that time, too. I thought I could cheer myself up by watching light, fluffy sitcoms on TV. But as I lay there on the couch, I found myself crying with every upbeat, cheery theme song that came with them. *Laverne and Shirley* making their dreams come true. *One Day at a Time*, which advised me to get up on my feet because somewhere there was music playing. And, oh, *Mary Tyler Moore*. Love is all around. My ass.

After that, it was a long, slow slide to my major breakdown. It wasn't unrelieved misery. I got married. I got a master's degree and a job in publishing. We acquired a house and cats. We traveled. But the Big One was waiting for me.

Nowadays, I still have mini-meltdowns, but they usually last a maximum of three days, rather than weeks, months, or even years. They still tend to be triggered by stressful life events, especially financial ones. But when I get one, I know I'll be coming out of it soon. And that's a wonderful feeling buried in all the misery.

Family Matters

NO ONE IN MY family understands me.

Actually, no one in my family understands my illness.

My mother-in-law doesn't believe that mental illness exists. And in a way she has a point. If she hasn't experienced something, for her it *doesn't* exist. Most people are a bit like that sometimes. There are only a few varieties of broken arms, and when you've got one, you know it. When you're talking synapses and neurotransmitters, thoughts and feelings, it's obvious why "invisible illnesses" *aren't* obvious or well understood.

I didn't understand my disorder at first, either. I remember driving past a building with a sign: South Community Mental Health. I didn't know what I was feeling, but I was pretty sure it wasn't mentally healthy. I went in and began the journey.

My family had the following reactions when I told them I was going into therapy and when I first started taking medication:

Dad: Just as long as *I* don't have to go.

Mom: I've heard Prozac is a ticking time bomb.

Mom (later): I thought you would feel better after you found a good job.

Sister: Why should you spend $100 a month just to talk to someone?

I understand some of those reactions. Dad had heard about how psychologists blame parents for messed-up kids and he wasn't going to someone to be told *he* was crazy and a bad parent besides. And his fear was not that unreasonable. Dysfunctional kids often *do* come from dysfunctional families. But underlying my disorder was brain chemistry. I never asked him to join the couch gang.

Mom watched Phil Donahue. And there was at first over-prescribing of Prozac and suicides once the patients gained enough energy. Plus, she thought my depression and anxiety were reactive and would clear up when my living situation was more stable.

My sister, I don't know. I don't understand her either. I'm sure she has psychological problems too, of one sort or another. But I've been diagnosed, so I'm the crazy one.

My husband, who has a background in psychology, "got it" a little better once he stopped trying to "fix" me. But he never understood in a visceral way until he had his own first meltdown.

He still hasn't felt the rapid cycling, the constant roller coaster, the extreme physical and mental battering of going on and off medication after medication, hoping the next one will do more than make his hands shake worse or his memory turn into Swiss cheese.

Still, it's better to be partly understood than completely dismissed, and to have a family that *tries*. And to have a family of choice that does understand, because a lot of them are in the same leaky, patched boat.

I could have done a lot worse.

A Mother? Me?

AH, THE SHRIEKS of laughter and squeals of delight from playful children! They cut through me like a light saber through Jell-O. I'm hyper-sensitive to loud or high-pitched noises.

A while back, one of my blogging buddies was speculating on whether she wanted to or ought to have a child, despite her disorder. I have no answer or even advice for her, but here is what I think about motherhood and Bipolar Me.

When we got married, my husband really wanted to be a father someday. To tell the truth, I never gave it much thought really, since I had never expected to be married.

At that time in my life I was barely medicated and had a lot of meltdowns and breakdowns and up-and-down cycles ahead of me.

Looking back, I am glad that I never became a mother. The thought alone overwhelms me.

First of all, I would have been a really bad mother. It would have been unfair to a child to have a mother who would disappear into her room for days at a time, not communicate for weeks at a time, be depressed for months, or years, at a time. Not to mention not being able to enjoy anything. Put that person in charge of a live human child for 18+ years?

I know there must be people who do it, but I don't even really understand how non-bipolar people manage it.

Second, (and this is the part that is going to sound selfish to those people who feel that childless-by-choice women are all selfish) I needed all the resources I had to construct and reconstruct myself. As Gloria Steinem said, "I **did not see any way that I could possibly give birth to** someone else and also give birth to myself. Far from feeling guilty, it was the first time that I had taken responsibility for my own life."

I still am, after my most recent and most monumental breakdown, still trying to salvage what I can of my psyche, seeing what pieces still fit, and learning to live with the things that are no longer present, or maybe never were.

And I had all kinds of irrational thoughts on the subject of motherhood. The one time I thought about motherhood, it was because my father was dying, and I wanted him to see his grandchild if there was going to be one.

Also, I was terrified of losing myself. My husband had some issues of his own and was, let's say, way too close to his inner child. I thought he and a child would outnumber me and I would be the mean one, the killjoy, the Other.

As time went on, I grew less and less inclined to even be around babies or small children. And my husband would go into a funk if one of our friends had a baby. Eventually, he decided that if he wasn't going to be a father, he could be a mentor, a helper, a healer, to other children and former children. Maybe even his inner child.

Now having a child is no longer even a possibility. And I'm good with that.

Mr. Fix-It

Him: I just groomed the cat. I used a cat-a-comb.
Me: *total silence*
Him: Hey, honey! I just groomed the cat, with a cat-a-comb!
Me: *more silence*

I WAS DEPRESSED, and he was trying to cheer me up. Using the same joke that had gotten no response only seconds before. I don't know why he thought it would work better the second time.

Many men have the instinct that, when confronted with a problem, they will try to solve it. When something is broken, they will try to fix.

I wasn't broken, exactly, but I was deep in the Pit of Despair, aka the lower mood swing of my bipolar disorder. At that stage, I was immobilized, uncommunicative, and utterly humorless.

The fact that Dan had worked in hospitals and psychiatric facilities was actually a bad thing, despite what you might expect. He had run laughter therapy groups, he knew the jargon, and he sincerely wanted to be helpful.

But he didn't know, viscerally, what depression was like, how it felt in your body and mind and soul, how it damped down your personality and blunted your reactions, removing your ability to view life as anything other than miserable. Certainly not funny.

Later Dan learned all this when he experienced his own bout of clinical depression and became another one of my Prozac pals. But until then, he would occasionally come shrinking at me, until I had to tell him to stop. I could accept a hug, but not a joke or a "remedy."

But all that was early in our relationship and before I had begun to heal or even get proper treatment. And I literally would not have made it this far without Dan. I need him and likely always will.

When it's Pit of Despair time again, he checks on me to see if I need that hug, or some food, or a kind word, or just to be left alone. When I am better, he still does the cooking and shopping, and reminds me to eat regular meals and take showers and tells me I smell nice after I do. Sometimes he can coax me out of bed with a tape of *The Mikado* or out of the house with lunch at Frisch's. If I'm too nervous to drive to my appointments, he takes me. When I'm together enough to work, he keeps the house quiet and fixes food when I need a break and validates me for being able to bring in money, even when it's difficult.

But he can't fix me. And now he knows that.

Taking Turns

FOR THE PAST several days, I have been dealing with a husband in severe pain from osteoarthritis, plantar fasciitis, and back spasms.

I have driven him to Urgent Care, picked up prescriptions, provided him with a walking stick and a cane, set up a heating pad, researched his conditions on the computer, talked him through his exercises, and more. I wish I could do all this without getting cranky. I wish he would follow my advice more, especially when I tell him to see a doctor. But sometimes he's such a *guy*.

What I have been doing for him is nothing at all compared to what he did for me and how he supported me when I had my last breakdown, which lasted several years. He did everything. Shopping, pet care, cooking, paying bills, earning a paycheck. Not to mention loving me through the despair, irrational thinking, sobbing uncontrollably, immobilization, and all the rest.

He really took that whole "in sickness and in health" thing to heart. Now it's my turn to do likewise.

I am completely out of spoons. I will carry on anyway. He deserves it.

How a Cat Helped Me Stay Sane

ANY PET CAN HELP with mental health. But in my case, it was a cat.

I was living alone after a bad breakup that had shattered me, mind and spirit. After moving twice, once from another state and once from an apartment complex after I lost the job that paid for it.

I was damaged, and I was alone, in the upstairs of a small house in a small town. I asked my landlady if I could have a cat. She was dubious but said yes.

I found a cat at a shelter. She was an adult tortoiseshell calico named Bijou. She was small and shy and quiet. The first night I took her home, she slept across my throat.

We needed each other. I needed someone to care about, to focus my attention outward on. She needed someone to draw her out of her shell, to care for and about her.

We took it slowly. At first, she didn't like to be held. When I got home from work she would meet me at the door. I would pick her up, give her a quick kiss on the head, and set her right back down. Soon she learned that being held wasn't such a bad thing.

Since then I have never been without a cat.

And they have improved my mental health. Pets do that.

Pets entertain when we need distraction. They can make us smile and even laugh.

Petting them brings tactile comfort and purring offers a soothing sound.

Caring for a pet makes us feel needed. Even when we have a hard time caring for ourselves, a pet becomes a responsibility bigger than we are.

Losing a pet teaches us about the process of necessary grieving. Then getting another pet teaches us about the process of loving someone new, opening our hearts again.

Pets listen. They don't judge.

Pets communicate with us and teach us their personal language.

Pets are now being used as therapy animals and comfort animals for the anxious, the aged, prisoners, and psychiatric patients. The laws and policies regarding "assistance animals" are only just beginning to be enacted. They are far from catching up with the need.

Even visits with farm animals – lambs, chickens, and ponies – are fulfilling vital roles in people's lives.

I've written about "crazy cat ladies" and even identified myself as one. There is a stigma that goes along with the label, yet another kind of stigma that we would be better off without. Admittedly, we can become obsessed with our companion animals, even to an extent that is unhealthy. They can be burdens, and annoyances, and expenses.

There are some people, perhaps people with rage issues, for example, who should not own pets. Having pets is a choice that should only be made if they and you fit together well. We've all read the stories and seen the pictures online of people who abuse pets horribly. Now those are the ones that I consider crazy.

Pets may not me be the right choice for other reasons. A person who travels a lot, or has extended hospital stays, may not be able to make the commitment. Germaphobes and emetophobes may not be able to handle the inevitable messes that come with pets. Even pet fish need their bowls cleaned.

Personally, I would avoid fish, unless the care of, say, tropical fish fascinates you. And their placid swimming can be calming. But for most of us, a pet that interacts with us is preferable. Birds aren't very cuddly, but they make agreeable sounds. Reptiles have their own fascination and aficionados. Me, I want something I can pet.

I don't think it's too much of a stretch to say that they are as much a part of my support system as I am theirs.

Chapter 5: Heavy Weather

On the Inside • Suffering and Train Wrecks • Cutters • Missing Friends • The Myth of Closure • What Was I Thinking? • The Wrong Life • The Week of Living Alone • Reaching the End of My Cope • Struggles and Tears • What Bipolar Disorder Has Cost Me • The Comfort That Remains

On the Inside

I SAW A pass-along the other day.

It reminded me of a lot of things. Things I try not to remember.

Not all scars show. Some of mine do. The one where kids threw a rock at me, requiring three stitches in my forehead. And the ones where I cut myself.

Others don't. I've often described my relationship with Rex as a train wreck. People wonder why I haven't gotten over it, all these years later. It was the sort of train wreck in which you lose pieces of yourself, some of them irreplaceable. These scars aren't the visible kind.

Not all wounds heal. Especially the wounds that happen when you're too young to know how to treat them. Cutting words. Emotional bruises. Neglect. Loneliness. There are no bandages that can cover them, no ointments that can soothe them, no miracle cures.

Not all illness can be seen. If we're high-functioning or have learned enough coping mechanisms, others may not notice. But bipolar disorder and other mental illnesses are, if not immediately visible, lurking just below the surface. And ready to break through at any time.

Not all pain is obvious. But it can leak out, especially around the eyes.

Remember this before passing judgment on another. But judgment-passing is practically an Olympic sport these days, along with shaming.

Scars. Wounds. Illness. Pain. These are things that those of us with mental disorders know all too well. What if our conditions are chemical imbalances in our brains? The consequences of having them, the misunderstandings they cause, the messages we receive, the behaviors we can't understand or control or mimic, the friends we lose, the opportunities and joys we miss out on, are very real. And don't let anyone tell you different.

Our disorders may be in our brains, but they're not all in our heads.

But you knew that, didn't you?

Suffering and Train Wrecks

WHAT DOESN'T KILL YOU makes you stronger.

Right.

This is one of the world's biggest falsehoods, right up there with "Sticks and stones may break my bones, but words will never hurt me."

It's a platitude we hear all the time, particularly those of us with mental illnesses.

And it's about time to call B.S. on the saying.

Suffering hurts. It grinds you down. It makes you less able to function. It keeps you from being the person you want to be.

Except in literature. There, suffering ennobles one, makes one a finer person, a more worthy person, and, yes, stronger. Once in a graduate-level literature class, I objected to this. I said the thing about suffering hurting and grinding you down. I got called a sociologist, which apparently is a terrible insult in literary circles. But they were talking about literature and I was talking about real life, so maybe we both had a point.

Back to the saying. There are lots of things that don't kill you, but also don't make you stronger. Train wrecks, for example. If they don't kill you, they can leave you on the brink of death or physically maimed or with PTSD. You may recover some, with help, but your back will still hurt, your leg won't regrow, and you can suffer from memories and dreams.

I've compared some relationships with train wrecks – most of us probably have. They simply cause you to suffer and the memories of them may always pain you like a damaged joint in bad weather. One can come through ordinary bad relationships and be stronger for it. But train wreck relationships, the toxic ones that erode your soul, do not ennoble or strengthen you.

Mental disorders can be like that. Yes, you may improve. Yes, you may become stronger in some ways. You may become more compassionate, more aware of others' pain, better able to avoid situations that will cause you harm, capable of rebuilding a different life with the parts you want to keep. But it's just as likely that when your brain breaks, it will never be good as new again. There will be cracks in your emotions or reasoning or moods that will be weaker, not stronger, and more likely to rupture again in the future.

We sufferers need strength, but it won't come from platitudes and bumper stickers.

And you can't explain this to people who haven't been there.

Also, don't get me started on that thing about God not giving you more than you can handle. We'd be here all week.

Cutters

If that title wasn't enough of a trigger warning, well, here goes:
TRIGGER WARNING: Self-Harm

CUTTING IS A REALITY that's mostly hidden from view.

Of course, it's not always cutting. Burning is popular too. But cutting is perhaps the most common name. There are websites devoted to it, some offering help, facts, and information on quitting (see below). But others glorify it as, I don't know, a creative expression of teen angst or something.

The name does keep changing. The last I heard, the "approved" psychiatric term was "Non-Suicidal Self-Injury" (NSSI). Self-mutilation, deliberate self-harm, non-fatal self-harm, self-destructive acts, self-inflicted violence, parasuicide, and self-wounding are all names for the dangerous practice performed by desperate people. The subject still isn't talked about much and carries a *huge* stigma. As if the mental and physical scars were not enough.

Some facts: Self-harm is not attempted suicide, though with some miscalculation it can lead to serious permanent injury or death. Most people associate it with teenage girls, but I've known at least one man in his 50s who cut himself regularly. It is not a matter of attention-seeking, since most cutters hide their physical wounds.

As I understand it, the practice results from one of two phenomena: the build-up of painful pressure such as perfectionism, or a feeling of severe alienation to the point of numbness. Cutting is a coping mechanism, though a dangerous, dysfunctional, and unsuccessful one, to deal with pain.

In my case, it was probably the numbness. I was feeling a lot of psychological pain in my college days, and irrationally wondered if physical pain would lessen that, or increase it, or feel any different. Like I said, irrational. All this was before I was diagnosed as bipolar, had a therapist, or was medicated.

I made a few small cuts on my wrist to watch the blood well up.

I wasn't suicidal. They weren't that kind of cuts. I do know the difference. It was more like when you stand on a bridge or balcony and look over the edge. You walk away. But you know the bridge is always there.

All told, I cut myself maybe three or four times. The scars are very faint now, white against my pale inner wrist, almost invisible. The memories are vivid. A friend who's a psychologist once asked me why I stopped. "Because I didn't need to anymore," was the only answer I could give. I've only felt the urge once since, and it was easy enough to push aside. But I recognized it.

I hesitated to write this, though I knew I would have to sooner or later, if I meant to share my experiences truthfully. One of my dearest friends once said that if he ever found out I was a cutter, I would never hear from him again. Except for his publicly mocking me for being so stupid.

Naturally, this sort of reaction, though common, is not helpful. I didn't tell him or practically anyone else. And I didn't tell him that at least two other people he knew, one fairly intimately, were also cutters.

Cutting isn't going away if we ignore it. It won't go away even if we do talk about it. Or mock it, or gasp in horror. But understanding self-injury is a big step.

If you're a cutter, or know someone who is, here are some places you can go for information, hope, and help:
- S.A.F.E. Alternatives (Self Abuse Finally Ends) – **http://www.selfinjury.com**
- Self-Injury and Related Issues (SIARI) – **http://www.self-injury.net**
- Recover Your Life (support community) – **http://www.RecoverYourLife.com**
- HelpGuide.org – **http://www.helpguide.org/mental/self_injury.htm**

Self-Harm Revisited

*If that title isn't enough of a **TRIGGER WARNING** for you, I don't know what is.*

NOT LONG AGO I saw on the web a video with the title "Is scratching self-harm?"

Well, of course it is, I thought.

The video agreed with me.

It seems like the low end of the spectrum, not as extreme as what most people think of as self-harm, but a form of it nonetheless. Scratching, pinching, hair pulling, and the like are probably considered subclinical next to cutting and burning. But they are still problems. They can escalate into worse self-harm.

In another article I saw this definition for self-harm: "Self-injury is intentional damage to body tissue (that doesn't include body modifications like piercings, tattoos, and scarification) without suicidal intent."

So, yes, scratching is self-harm. It is intentional. It is damage to body tissue. And it does not indicate suicidal intent.

Scratching sounds so minor. We scratch ourselves all the time when we have an itch or an insect bite. We scratch ourselves accidentally on protruding nails. Occasionally we draw blood. We wash it off, slap on a band-aid, and that's that.

But when scratching escalates to self-harm, it can indeed be serious. For one thing, scratches tend to become infected, infection of the sort can lead to further tissue damage and if untreated, to more serious complications.

There is also the potential for further harm because the scratching will scab over. Then the desire to scratch off the scab kicks in. When this happens, the scratches never heal. And yes, that's both a fact and a metaphor.

My own experience with scratching came when I was working at a job that required me to monitor burglar alarms. The alarms tended to go off during thunderstorms. When a storm hit, a dozen or more alarms could go off simultaneously, or at least in rapid succession. I had to call the owners of the businesses, or emergency services as required.

One night during a particularly bad storm, I missed one of the alarms. I did not call the owners until I looked back at the record. When I called, it was 45 minutes since the alarm. I knew I had made a mistake, and a bad one. The owners of the business would not be happy. My boss would not be happy. I was not happy.

I sat alone by the monitors and imagined the trouble I was in. I started scratching my right arm, long slow strokes from nearly the wrist to nearly the elbow. Repetitively. Obsessively. Painfully. I believe I was punishing myself for making a bad mistake. Perhaps there was some thought that if I inflicted the pain, I would escape further consequences of my mistake.

Of course, that makes no sense. It's an example of the irrational thinking that goes with self-harm.

I don't cut anymore, as I discussed earlier. I also don't scratch the way I did that night. I still tend to pick scabs. Occasionally if I have an insect bite, I will scratch it to blood and then pick the scabs on that. I try not to. My husband helps me by reminding me not to pick at scabs or to put band-aids on them. I try to rub instead of scratch or use lotion.

Jenny Lawson (aka the Bloggess) has admitted in her most recent book, *Furiously Happy*, that she scratches past the point of bleeding and pulls her hair enough to create bald spots. It's clear that she considers this self-harm. Her husband tries to help her with it too.

But self-harm is basically a private thing – something we do and hide from the world. Some people can hide it even from their most intimate family and loved ones. I know I wore long sleeves to cover the dreadful scratch on my right arm. It healed from a scratch to a pink scar and then to a white scar. Now I can't even see it anymore through the freckles.

But I don't need the visible reminder. I remember how it felt to do it, how it felt after I did it, and how I felt as I watch the scars slowly fade. It's nothing I'm proud of, except for the fact that I survived it and no longer do it.

As most cutters and other people who self-harm do, I feel shame in recalling the act, and almost never speak of it. The reason I'm sharing the story in such a public forum is to let people know that not all self-harm consists of big dramatic gestures. It can start with a tiny scratch. But it is not something to be ignored. We need to talk about self-harm, educate about it, bring it out in the open, and let others know that it doesn't have to continue.

And that it can start with something as small as a scratch.

Missing Friends

EARLIER I WROTE about the controversial subject of self-harm. In my post, I said:

"One of my dearest friends once said that if he ever found out I was a cutter, I would never hear from him again. Except for his publicly mocking me for being so stupid."

I had withheld a part of my past from someone with whom I have practically no secrets, sometimes to the point of TMI. Finally. I tired of wondering whether he had read the post.

I called him and asked, "Are we OK?"

At first, he didn't know what I meant, since he hadn't read the post, but after a brief nudge I could tell he knew exactly what I was referring to.

Just as a (very rational) mutual friend had predicted, he chalked it up to the hyperbole of his callow youth and reassured me that we were fine.

Still.

I had lived with the fear of losing that important relationship (and being publicly mocked) for over 20 years. I had never dared mention it to any people in our circle either.

And, let's face it, I have lost other friends and can attribute at least some of these losses to my bipolar disorder. It harms me, but it also harms those around me, and especially relationships.

I have shot my mouth off and driven away friends and colleagues with bitterness and sarcasm but without realizing how I sounded.

I have ratted out a friend to his therapist and his wife when he was suicidal, which he found unforgivable.

I have turned down invitations to go out or agreed to and then backed out one too many times. My friend gave up the effort since I wasn't responding.

I have abused the hospitality of friends. When I was still functioning moderately well, I would visit, and we would enjoy activities, food, conversation, and music. When I was near or at the depths, I would invite myself to visit and turn into an uncommunicative, disengaged, immobilized lump. I was a moocher and a leech, and a real downer generally. I didn't like spending time with myself, so it's no wonder they didn't either.

And I miss every single one of them. I wish I hadn't driven them away. I wish I could make things right again, now that I'm functioning at a higher level. But I can't. And that hurts.

In some cases, I've tried to make things right, even sent brief notes of apology. They have been acknowledged, if at all, with cold politeness that does not invite more contact. I don't know what else I can do.

Bipolar is a cyclical illness and, though I'm much improved, I can't promise that I will never sink that low, be that inconsiderate, offend those I deeply care about again. And I can't blame them for not wanting to deal with that. *I* don't want to deal with it.

But I have no choice in the matter. And that hurts too.

Fortunately, there's one friend I cannot lose, no matter what – my husband. He's ridden the roller coaster with me, put up with the huge mood swings, ignored the irrational remarks, offered to help in any way, encouraged me to go out but understands when I can't, and dispensed hugs on a regular basis. He respects alone time and is there when I need company or distraction. If things are bad, he gets me to eat and helps me shower and takes care of the pets and picks up my refills and does whatever else needs doing.

He's a man who takes "in sickness and in health" seriously. I wouldn't have made it this far without him. And I won't ever lose him, till death do us part.

The Myth of Closure

FOR SOME REASON, it's called "closure." But for some wounds there is no such thing. And for some of us – those with emotional and mental disorders – there is no way to achieve closure.

Take, for example, the invisible injuries I experienced while living with Rex for a year in college. He was a master of intermittent reinforcement, the trap that keeps abused women and men from getting themselves out of the situation to someplace safe. He was never physically abusive, which I have vowed never to put up with, but verbally and emotionally, he was, well, a veritable artist of psychological bullying.

Here are just a few examples.

When he was unhappy with me for some reason, he would sigh and glare. I swear he could sigh and glare even over the telephone. And when I would freeze up and not be able to think of any words that would make things better, he said my silence made him want to kick me.

I slept in the car on the streets of Buffalo if there was a late-night party he wanted to go to. It was out of the way for him to take me back to where we were staying.

When I was responsible for feeding guests, and botched it, he said I had tarnished his honor.

He took the decision to tell my parents about our relationship out of my hands, ripping apart the face-saving fiction that I was renting a room in his large house. After I left, I even sent him money to pay the supposed rent.

When I asked him to go to couples' counseling with me, he said, "Are you sure? The therapist and I could have you declared a danger to yourself and have you put away."

At the session, he tenderly held my hand and asserted that he just wanted to get help for me.

So, what does this all have to do with mental health? I certainly wasn't mentally healthy when I met him and was a basket case by the time I left. When I was immobilized, I was not embracing his projects with "alacrity." When I was insomniac, only his cat comforted me. When I was in the Pit of Despair, everything was All My Fault.

What do people tell you in cases like this?

Look how much you learned from the experience. And I always reply that the lesson wasn't worth the price I paid. All that I want to keep from that time are a few dear friends.

Forgive and forget. I can't do either. The memories have faded over time and seldom give me flashbacks anymore. (The dreams still come.) As for forgiving? He's never asked for it and never would. I'm sure he doesn't think he did anything that needed forgiving. If that makes me a hard-hearted bitch or a bad Christian, so be it.

That emotional abuse happened, and I *can't* forget it. It was my first serious relationship and I left chunks of my soul and most of my barely existent self-esteem in that house on the hilltop. I had failed at the relationship, at meeting my parents' expectations, at so many things. I felt I was the one who needed forgiveness and spent much of the following years repeating incessantly, "I'm sorry."

Let go of anger; it will only hurt you. When I first left, I didn't feel anger toward Rex. I felt a lot of other things, mostly directed at myself. But I didn't recognize or own my anger until much later, after lots of therapy and the good kind of love. Now that I realize I was, and still am, angry, it feels wrong to think of him without feeling that. The things he did were wrong, and it is not irrational of me to still believe that. I earned that anger. It is part of me now.

I can lay it aside to the extent that I don't have revenge fantasies, but that's about all.

So, closure? Not a chance. Saying as Oscar Wilde did, "Living well is the best revenge"? That's more like it. Even learning to live well has been an uphill battle. I'm still struggling with the definition.

The wound may scab over, or it may continue to trickle blood at times. Some of it may even form scars. But take my word for it, the wounds are still there. They never close.

What Was I Thinking?

WHEN I WAS A KID, I had irrational thoughts all the time. I think most kids do. They were harmless, even amusing.

It's when you're older that they become problems, or even dangers.

Looking back, my irrational thoughts were almost all fears.

My younger self wouldn't eat rhubarb because I knew that some part of the plant was poisonous, and I didn't want to take a chance. I still don't eat rhubarb. Any vegetable that needs that much sugar to make it palatable hardly seems worth it. I suppose that could be considered an early OCD-type thought, since it was about potentially toxic food.

Another irrational fear was based on the fact that I had no idea how plumbing really worked. I was afraid that if I flushed the toilet right before I brushed my teeth, the waste water somehow flowed past the tap and could end up on my toothbrush.

Yet another plumbing-related misconception dealt with sex, but we won't go into that now. Let's just say they never covered it in health class back then. For all I know, they still don't. I had my mother buy me a copy of *Everything You Always Wanted to Know About Sex but Were Afraid to Ask* so I could find the answer.

In my teen years, my irrational thoughts became more delusional, and more related to my by-then-shaky mental health. At some point it was recommended that I should visit a counselor. And they were right. I certainly should have, although in retrospect, child psychiatry in those days was primitive and I most likely wouldn't have received a correct diagnosis or treatment. I don't think bipolar type 2 even existed.

I'll say this for my parents: They consulted me on whether I wanted to go or not, which was not what I would have expected them to do. I declined.

My "reason"? I somehow thought that having such a thing on my permanent record would keep me from getting into a good, or perhaps any, college. When I started applying, of course, no one even asked.

And once I was in college and knew that my sanity was truly on shaky ground, my life goal was to graduate, and then work enough quarters at pretty much anything until I qualified for Social Security before I was put away. I was convinced that was likely to be my fate. I'm not sure why I thought that having Social Security would have helped.

None of those irrational fears was ever addressed in a timely manner. Except the sex one. Yay, me! for finding some accurate information on that one and Yay, Mom! for facilitating my enlightenment.

If you've noticed a trend of increasing irrationality and increasing potential for sabotaging my own life, you're not wrong.

*** TRIGGER WARNING ***

The rest of this is tough stuff. You know what's coming, so stop now if you're not ready to hear about it.

When I had my major meltdown 10 or so years ago, I had the worst irrational thought of all. My mother had just died, so my thought processes were scrambled anyway.

Then my husband did something that I thought was unethical and likely illegal as well. Then he said he'd do it again if he had to. I managed to talk our way out of the first instance as a simple mistake, but his statement that he might do it again haunted me.

I catastrophized, of course. This time, however, the potential catastrophe loomed large and to me very real. If he did repeat his actions, there would be no possibility of smoothing things over. He would be culpable. And I would be in the position of needing to report it.

Then he would lose his job, at the very least, which was at the time loosely related to the legal system. They wouldn't be able to overlook it.

I was unable to work at the time, trying to get disability, and we were barely staying afloat. Without his job, we would sink.

So, I thought that, if he did it again, and I reported it, and he lost his job, the only thing left for me to do was kill myself.

Like I said, irrational.

I had a plan, though. In fact, I had three or four different plans and I couldn't decide among them. Indecision is part of what kept me alive.

As it turns out, my husband did not choose to repeat his actions, and I was spared the necessity of choosing among mine.

Soon thereafter, I got help. I never mentioned the suicidal thoughts till they were long gone, so I never even had to fear the dreaded lock-up that I had anticipated all those years before.

I kept one of the intended means of exit for a while, though. Just in case.

It was a major day in my healing when I finally let that go. That irrational thought had been dismissed and conquered.

The Wrong Life

NOTHING PREPARED ME for this.

This is not the life my upbringing prepared me for. I don't just mean the special guest speakers we had in home economics class who tried to introduce us to the subtleties of silver, china, and stemware. No, I was also misled by the books I read.

If Life Is a Bowl of Cherries, What Am I Doing in the Pits? and *Please Don't Eat the Daisies* led me astray. Don't get me wrong, I'm a total fan of Erma Bombeck's writing style, but the quirky suburban life she loved and lamented was not what I got. Bombeck and Kerr both made light, and fortunes, of portraying the petty foibles and cute misunderstandings of women and their husbands, women and their children, women and their neighbors, women and other women.

Daily disasters with dishwashers, sticky-fingered children, and clueless husbands were an endless source of amazement and amusement for them. They soldiered on, supported by an innate buoyancy, faith in the divinity, and the occasional glass of wine.

My glasses of wine have been more than occasional. My disasters have not been humorous. I do not have children, and the cats are somewhat deficient in making adorable conversation in high-pitched, lisping voices. Sometimes all I can get out of them is "meh," which is pretty much how I feel, too.

As for the trappings of the genteel life, we eat off paper plates more often than not. I did once have a set of Limoges, but only because I was acting as a pawnbroker for a friend who needed ready cash. I fed one of the cats on the Limoges saucer, just to say that I had.

My parents used to say that their house was decorated in Early Married Junk and I have followed in that fine tradition. Most of our furnishings are a demonstration of the maxim: If it's not from Kmart or Goodwill you won't find it here.

No one's life prepares them for clinical depression, hypomania, bipolar disorder, or any other mental illnesses. I'll wager that even psychologists' kids don't have a clue when they escalate from picking scabs to experimenting with lit cigarettes. Maybe their parents don't either.

Either the mental disorder has been going on so long that you don't know what it's like without it, or it comes on so suddenly that you desperately hope that it goes away just as suddenly. Or it comes in a way that you can just convince yourself is no big deal. "I overspend? That's just because I love shopping, not because I have mania or need to validate myself with expensive things."

Perhaps people who grow up with a mentally disturbed loved one have a chance of understanding the underlying mechanisms. But with the number of families who don't discuss the elephant in the room, or pass it off as, "Your sister is just high-strung" or say, "Uncle Ted is a little odd. Just ignore him," not even that exposure may help.

How do young people learn about mental illness? Or even (gasp!) get help for one? If not at home, maybe at school? The National Association of Secondary School Principals cites the U.S. Surgeon General's report saying that "one in five children and adolescents will face a significant mental health condition during their school years" and that the ratio of school counselors to students is 471:1. Add to that the fact that most school counselors have been shifted away from offering personal and emotional support to offering academics-only services.

Most of us struggle alone. Some never find a proper diagnosis and treatment. We must be our own resources and our own advocates much of the time, even if our illnesses do not allow us to get out of bed. If we have one family member, or even a close friend, who understands, we are lucky beyond measure.

I wish that I had been even slightly prepared for the life I now lead, instead of the one I was "supposed" to have. No one can predict the future, but why can't we at least have a bit of mental health education in school? I suppose that's a lot to ask, when even sexuality education varies from the merely adequate to the appalling, when schools are barely able to stay abreast of the teach-to-the-test curriculum, and when Texas's governor vetoes a bipartisan bill allocating resources for mental health, based on lobbying by Scientologists.

Do I sound bitter because I didn't get to live the genteel suburban life? Probably. But there are aspects of that life that likely would have actively impeded my search for mental health. So, I've had to do it on my own, or nearly so, at least until recently. A lot of us go DIY for mental health.

But a lot of us are accomplishing it. Living the life we have and not some fictitious pie-in-the-sky one. We may not have been prepared for it, but we muddle through anyway and sometimes even realize that imperfect real life is better than a perfect lie.

The Week of Living Alone

SOMETIMES, WHEN I get tired of my complicated life, I imagine what it would be like to start over someplace new, or what it might have been like if I had made different choices. I envision myself, living alone (well, with one cat), in a small town like Benson, AZ. I would have a small used bookstore or secondhand shop and live in a small apartment over it or behind it. I would have a couple of friends I met in my shop and go out to lunch or dinner occasionally, but mostly spend my free time listening to music, watching TV, or on the Internet.

Sounds simple and peaceful, doesn't it?

This past week has convinced me that even such a stripped-down existence would not be possible for me. My husband was out of town for nine days, and I could barely manage.

Those of you who have read this far know that my husband is my rock and my support. I often say I could not get through without him, and my recent experiences only reinforce that.

I didn't begrudge his leaving, though I wish he had not been gone quite that long. His mother needed him to help her get ready to sell her house and move, and nine days was barely enough time to start on all that needed to be done. There are times she needs him as much as I do.

But coping on my own was difficult. I have paid work I have to do. It matches perfectly with my skill-set and I'm grateful to have it, but sometimes it's just plain hard to do and hard to make myself do. And I have two blogs (bipolarjan.wordpress.com and janetcobur.wordpress.com) that I have made a commitment to posting once a week. Plus, I have started writing a mystery novel.

We have four cats, two of them ancient, and one dog, also ancient. I was afraid that one of them might die while my husband was away. Thankfully none did.

As scary as the idea of coping with a dying or dead animal on my own was, just caring for them was difficult. They keep demanding food several times a day, you see, and they have no thumbs to open cans with. Then there's the water bowls and the litter boxes. I used to live alone with one cat and manage okay, but that was many years and many meltdowns ago.

Then there was feeding me. Dan had stocked up on things I like before he left, but after the French bread pizzas were gone, I lived largely on salami sandwiches, cheese and crackers, and cereal. I also had a small tray of sliced veggies and dip. Once I made a couple of baked frozen fish sandwiches early in the week, but later I had devolved to the extent that my evening meal was peanut butter on a bagel. Another night I had mashed potatoes and a glass of red wine. Other meals I simply skipped.

Then there was Dealing with Stuff. Life Stuff. You know. The Stuff that happens to everyone sometimes piled up on me. I had to talk to (argue with) the utility company and the IRS. I had to pay bills. Life Stuff leaves me exhausted.

Plus, I kept having to Go Out. Deposit my check. See the doctor. Pick up prescriptions. Buy cat food when I ran out. I wore pants more days last week than I had in the previous month. Dan wanted me to water his butterfly garden daily, but it rained every day or night, so I didn't have to put on pants and go out for that. I treated myself to lunch twice when I had to go out to do those errands, but it was nearly impossible to decide where to eat.

Now Dan is back. I had to put on pants again, so we could return his rental car.

But you see what I'm getting at here.

My fantasy of retreating to a simpler life is not feasible. It simply wouldn't work. The everyday tasks and trials of managing a shop, caring for myself and a pet, negotiating all the stuff of life would overwhelm me. Oh, when I'm hypomanic and can sometimes focus, I might do all right for a while, but life, even a very basic one, would eventually overwhelm me. There are so many things I can no longer do, at least not without serious amounts of help and support.

I can muddle through for a while mostly on my own. I am getting better. But not better enough to live independently, at least not right now.

Reaching the End of My Cope

ANYMORE, I DON'T very often have days when I can't get out of bed, but this week I had one. It doesn't matter now what caused it, but I am feeling the lingering after effects. Today I had no choice but to get out of bed, and I thought as long as I'm up, I might as well blog.

I had been headed for bed-bound all week. The slowly creeping whelms; the feeling of being nibbled to death by mice; the recent trauma of two pets' deaths; a game I couldn't win, couldn't break even, and couldn't get out of. Expected relief came three days too late.

Aside from not eating, not getting out of bed meets many of my needs of quiet, rest, naps, not having to fight off the numbness and care about anything. And yes, there's some feeling sorry for myself in there too. I won't try to deny it. Staying in bed is a big messy wad of self-pity, anhedonia, lack of energy, trying to stave off thoughts, and generally not being able to give a shit about anything. It is more than sadness. It is as J.K. Rowling described the Dementors: You feel as if you will never be happy again. In other words, there's nothing worth getting out of bed *for*.

When I was searching for images to go with this post, I entered "end of rope." I guess I expected to see cute kittens dangling and inspirational quotes like "Hang on, Baby, Friday's Coming!"

Instead, what I found were endless images of nooses. Nooses by themselves or with people in them. Overturned chairs under nooses. Photos, illustrations, every conceivable image of nooses. According to the visual imagination of illustrators and photographers, "end of one's rope" meant suicide. There were some images of frayed or broken ropes, but the nooses were in the lead by at least four to one.

That's not what I mean by "end of my rope," not dangling kittens OR nooses. Staying in bed all day, being unable to function, is a long, long way from suicide. Indeed, I find it a mechanism that staves off thoughts of nooses. Staying in bed admits of the possibility that tomorrow, or maybe the next day, I will have the wherewithal to drag myself out of that bed. Or that something will force me out of the bed and I will have to respond, as it happened today.

Hence the title of this piece. I have not reached the end of my rope, certainly not to find a dangling noose at the end of it. I have not reached the end of my hope, because I believe that someday, I hope soon, I will be out of the bed and at least as far as the sofa, and then who knows?. But when I stay in bed all day, I have reached the end of my cope.

This is not exactly the same as reaching the end of my spoons, because I don't use up any spoons by lying in bed. And I don't really know, or perhaps don't believe, that I will have a new supply the next day.

I expect that some people will beat me up for being so useless as to give up for even a day, to be unable even to try. I know I'm beating myself up over it too. But today I am out of bed, for at least part of the day, and I am writing. That means there's at least an inch of rope left. An inch of cope.

Struggles and Tears

IN THE PAST WEEK I have had to deal with:

- My husband being out of town
- Said husband driving home for 10 hours with faulty brakes
- My insurance company going belly-up
- My meds running out before new insurance could be implemented
- My cat going missing
- My check being late, so I could not pay mortgage, pay new insurance, pay for meds, pay power bill
- Being immobilized and unable to leave the house

Out of all of those, which do you think came nearest to breaking my brain, causing me to catastrophize and dissolve into prolonged fits of weeping?

If you guessed the missing cat, you're right. One day she trotted out the deck door while I was feeding the dog, a thing she had never done before. I scooped her up and put her back inside and resolved to close the door further in the future. Louise is 20 and rather thin, so it's easy to misjudge what she can squeeze through.

When my husband got back (safely), he took over feeding the dog. Then the next day, Louise didn't show up for her morning breakfast. Or lunch. Or dinner. She usually has a hearty appetite and meows quite loudly if a meal is late.

Naturally, I thought she had gotten outside again and was lost. We searched through the house, calling her name, and went around outside the house doing likewise. My husband thought she might be feeling poorly and holed up somewhere, most likely in the basement, which is also the garage and not easy to search because of all the clutter.

I thought she must have gotten out and succumbed to some fate out in the woods – a dog or other animal, the rain, hunger, illness and debilitation.

I was convinced she was gone for good. And I had thought I still had more time with her, despite her advanced age (20+). I was inconsolable. My precious cat, gone. No knowing what had happened to her. No chance to say goodbye. No way to comfort her in her last hours on earth.

Dan told me that everything would be all right, but I didn't believe him.

Then, the next day, she showed up at mealtime, bellowing that she wanted food NOW! Dan had been right. She had hidden somewhere in the house and came out when she was ready to. I had my darling Louise back, for however long she still has.

Then, after the long holiday weekend, the check came, and I paid the bills and set up the new insurance and got my meds and went out to lunch with Dan and everything was all right.

Just a little while ago, I wrote about how having a cat saved my sanity and how they can be good for people with mental disorders. I even said that losing a pet could teach us something about the grieving process.

But when my own cat disappeared, all that philosophizing went out the window or the deck door. Louise was gone, and I was bereft. Nothing anyone could say could make it better. And the situation was complicated by the fact that both one of our other cats and our dog are also ancient. I know I will go through their loss, and likely soon.

Will I hold up any better?

I really don't know. The other cat and the dog are my husband's, bonded to him the way Louise is bonded to me. Likely, his grief will be greater than mine. Or maybe when they pass they will remind me of how close I came to losing Louise. Maybe I'll be able to support him in his loss, or maybe my brain will break again. Maybe it will happen when I am more stable, with fewer disasters and near-disasters clustering around my head.

That's the thing with pets. You never know how long you have with them. You never know whether you'll be relatively stable when you have to face their loss.

But I know I won't give them up. The loneliness of not having them is even worse than the pain of their going.

What Bipolar Disorder Has Cost Me

WE LOSE A LOT when we live with bipolar disorder – function, memory, friends and even family.

But we also lose something more tangible – money. Or at least I did, and I know that a number of others have experienced this as well. Here's how it went for me.

Work. I quit my full-time office job, possibly in a fit of hypomania. I had a new boss and had told her about my disorder. Her only question was, "What will that mean?"

My answer was, "Sometimes I'll have good days and bad days."

Immediately after that, I began receiving bad evaluations, which I never had before. Was my performance really declining? It probably was, as I was heading into a major depressive episode.

But I wasn't out of work quite yet. For a while I worked freelance, and pretty successfully. Then my brain broke, and there I was, unemployed. I had savings in a 401K, and we ran through all of that. Then my husband had a depressive episode and we ran through his 401K as well. And the money we got from refinancing our house.

Disability. Sometime in that stretch of time, my husband realized that our money was going to run out. He asked me to file for disability. Many of you know that story. I was denied. I got a disability lawyer. By this time, years later, I was able to work freelance again a bit, and my lawyer told me shortly before my appeal hearing was scheduled that the hearing officer's head would explode when he learned what my hourly rate was.

Never mind that I could work only a few hours a week, maybe five in a good week.

Insurance. Then there was insurance. As a freelancer, of course, I didn't have any. My husband's good county job had covered us, until he became unemployed too. I'm sure a lot of you know that story as well. No insurance. Huge pharmacy bills, and psychiatrist and psychotherapist, and doctor visits and the odd trip to Urgent Care.

Meds. Then my doctor put me on Abilify, $800 a month. I got a couple of months free from the drug company, just enough to discover that it really worked for me and I didn't want to give it up.

Then, with remarkable timing, the Affordable Care Act (aka Obamacare) came along and we were able to get insurance again. It wasn't really affordable, though, costing only slightly less per month than the Abilify. But it covered all our other prescriptions, too, so we came out a little ahead.

Budget. Since then, that's the way it's been going, month to month and disaster to disaster. My work is irregular, and I never know how much I'll get in any given month. My husband's pay is steady, but meager – minimum wage or just a smidge above. We have managed to make our mortgage payments and keep the house, which my husband doubted we'd be able to do when I couldn't work. I know in that respect, we're way luckier than many families struggling with bipolar disorder.

Our latest disaster came this week, when our only remaining partially working vehicle blew out second gear as well as well as the already blown reverse. The money we had borrowed and put aside for major dental work that the insurance wouldn't cover disappeared with a poof, and still wasn't enough. We had to borrow more from an already fed-up relative. I don't blame her. She never expected to have to keep bailing out her grown son and his wife when she herself was past retirement age.

Our Future. I don't see anything changing. My mental disorder is under much better control, but I know I'll never be able to work in a full-time 9–5 job again. Job opportunities are few for people our age anyway, despite anti-age-discrimination laws. And I've never tried applying for a job where I must ask for accommodations to offset my illness, but I'm sure employers find lots of reasons not to hire people who need those. Again, despite the laws.

So why am I telling you all this? Am I just whining and feeling sorry for myself? Well, yes, I am, but that's not the point, really. Bipolar disorder takes a brutal toll on our emotional lives, our families, our relationships, and more. It can also put us on the brink of poverty, or in our case, one paycheck and one more disaster away from desperate straits. I know that there are bipolar sufferers, including some of my friends, in much worse straits.

It's stressful.

And we all know how stress affects a person with bipolar disorder.

Badly.

The Comfort That Remains

HERE I AM, caught between reactive depression and clinical depression.

I've been having a rough month. Several months. It's been a real challenge to my hard-won quasi-stability.

Last week, my 20+ year old cat, Louise died. The week before that, my husband's 17+ year old cat died. Then our 17-year-old dog died. So now I am trying to deal with those reactive feelings of grief and loss, without losing myself in the eternally waiting Pit of Despair that is clinical depression.

In doing that, I am trying to find things that remain to take comfort in.

I take comfort that my husband was here with me, to help me through.

That Louise had a good, long life spent in our loving care since she was a tiny kitten.

That she died peacefully, at home, in my lap, with me petting her.

That I had a chance to say goodbye to her.

That I know she loved me as much as I loved her.

That her presence and her purr helped calm me and helped me when nothing else could.

That she gave me a constant presence through a third of my life, and all of hers.

We have two cats now – Dushenka and Toby. They are young and healthy, but of course our time with them is not guaranteed. I know that, just by having them and loving them, we are inviting future grief into our lives, along with the joy. That's just how it is.

I've been reflecting a lot lately on animals, humans, and what we share with each other. It's hard. Is it harder when your brain doesn't work right and tries to tell you that sorrow doesn't end?

I don't know. There's no scale by which to compare pain, and loss, and despair, and grief. We each go through it the only way we can.

I hope that soon, at least a few of the clouds will part and I can feel something besides sorrow, express something other than pain. Maybe next week's blog will be about healing, or coping, or sharing strengths.

Those are all things I need to be doing, that we all need to be doing.

Someone remarked this week that a recent post was not about healing. It reflected, the commenter said, all the privileges I have: money, drugs I can take to help me through a crisis, a supportive husband. And that's all true. I have these privileges and more besides: a home, work that I can do without leaving the house, insurance, a psychiatrist and a psychotherapist. Some of these come to me because of circumstances I don't control, and some I have had to work very hard for, as I have worked hard for the ability to heal, a little bit at a time.

There are still things I cannot do: leave the house more than twice a month or so, shop for groceries, see the dentist without massive panic, stop taking the psychotropic meds that allow me to think, have a healthy sexual relationship. I expect that some of these will get better and others won't.

But, no matter our symptoms or their severity, we as people with bipolar disorder are all in this together, or, as the Bloggess would say, alone together. Maybe I have an easier time of it, but that's far from saying it's easy for me.

I still experience grief and sorrow, depression and anxiety, irrationality and immobilization, pain and despair, relief and help, struggle and hard work, love and loneliness.

And always, I look for the comfort that comes when I need it most, or expect it least, or believe I'll never feel again. We all do.

Chapter 6: Swings Go Both Ways

The Hypomanic Blogger • Ack! Ack! • From Panicky to Manicky • Maybe Another Manic Monday • The Fragility of Hypomania • Out of the House – At Last! • I Got Away Successfully! • Looking Back – But How Far? • Beware the Mental Health Meme

The Hypomanic Blogger

WHEN I THOUGHT I had unipolar depression, I used to wish I were bipolar, on the theory that I could get a lot more done. I later found that not to be true, as I'm sure many of you can attest.

I had a lot more experience with depression than with mania. My bipolar disorder is Type 2, which means I get hypomania instead of full-blown mania. And most of the time the hypomania comes out sideways as anxiety and/or irritability.

Don't ask me why I get the full-Monty-style depression and only a smidge of hypomania. I don't know. If my shrink does, he hasn't told me.

Looking back, I can remember only one hypomanic episode before my new diagnosis made me more aware of the possibility. I was working at writing and editing, the same things I do now, only then I could do it in an office full-time instead of at home and freelance. A woman came to me, asking about how she could become a writer for magazines.

I positively burbled and babbled. I gave her all sorts of advice on query letters and *Writer's Market* and niche publications and getting bylines and clips. I told her about how I started, writing for *I Love Cats* magazine and editing my martial arts club's journal, and working my way up. Incidentally, I am, as far as I know, the only person ever to have articles published in both *Black Belt* and *Catechist* magazines.

The woman went away inspired, she said, though I never heard how she made out.

Now I can more easily recognize hypomania when it hits. I still get the anxious and irritable sort, but now I get more of the buzzy kind. And even though it makes me twitchy, I can make use of it.

It was in a bout of hypomania that I decided to start this blog and my other, general-purpose one – janetcobur.wordpress.com. It's hypomania that has kept me going for over two years so far. I can now, thanks to medication, force myself to work while in the dysthymic stage or the "meh" stage. If I hit a spell of hypomania, I can use it to write and edit. Right now, I'm using a hypomanic swing to stockpile ideas and first drafts against the inevitable downswing.

Of course, the ramblings that go with hypomania are not worth posting or submitting to a client the way they hit the screen. When I'm less jazzed, but not in the Pit of Despair, I can re-read, edit, and improve. It's a fine balance, a tightrope I'm learning to walk. And it takes both therapy and medication to maintain.

In essence the not-properly-treated bipolar 2 made my work go downhill, until I was unable to work at all. Now that my diagnosis and my meds are more on track, so am I. I may not be well, but I certainly am better. I can live with what I've got, and even re-learn how to use some of the abilities I lost in my most recent, largest, most devastating crash.

I wouldn't recommend mania or even hypomania to anyone, but as long as I've got it, I might as well make it be good for something.

Ack! Ack!

OH NOES! Another business meeting/training session/lunch!
On Wednesday, not much time to get ready.
Panic? Check.
Hair appointment? Check.
Therapist appointment? Check.
Everything else? Not check.
Will I ever be able to do this again without freaking out? Guess that's a question for my therapist.

Bonus Material (Actual Conversation):
Me (distraught): I have to find something to wear!
Husband (helpful): What about that white thing you wore last time?
Me (gently): It's June, and that was a turtleneck with long sleeves.
Husband (no particular tone of voice): Oh.

I didn't bother explaining that it was actually off-white and I couldn't wear the same thing to two of these events in a row. The seasonal thing was a big enough information bite.

From Panicky to Manicky

I'VE BEEN HAVING one of my rare, slightly manicky upswings for the last few days.

Why? And about what?

Well, I survived the business meeting/lunch on Wednesday. I prepared for it with a lot less anxiety than the last time (hair, outfit, jewelry, car, arrival time – all came together with astonishing speed). I even made it through lunch without my hand tremors causing me to dibble all over myself. Yay me!

And although the subject matter could have felt like an attack directed at me, it didn't. I didn't get defensive (well, maybe a little) and I help uncover some problems that indirectly supported my point of view.

Also, I was not completely spoon-depleted that evening or the next day, as I had told my husband to expect.

I've donated small amounts of money ($25 and under) to a few charities and causes. I don't know if this is cause or effect of the upswing, but who cares? I was motivated, and I did it. A small enough accomplishment for many people but summoning the will to care and to act constitutes progress.

I have supported a friend in his first solo freelance venture, predicted its astoundingly rapid success, and reveled in it with him. It's a good feeling to share, even if my own freelance efforts have been less spectacular (though significant to me).

I won't deny that this upswing makes me wary that a crash may be on the way. You know how feeling happy always seems like tempting fate? With bipolar disorder, I know that there will always be another downswing waiting around the corner for me.

But at least, for now, I can enjoy the good. And that's a major improvement.

Maybe Another Manic Monday

THE GREAT ABILIFY experiment is underway. I'm still roller-coastering, which is "normal" for me, but I really can't tell whether the drug is affecting the ups and downs.

The highs and lows do seem to be higher and lower (respectively). I am dubious about this being a Good Thing. For several days I was so thoroughly depressed that I was ready to call Dr. R. and tell him I need to stop taking the drug. Then I leveled out to my usual place on the continuum: functioning, but not spectacularly well or consistently.

Now I think I'm starting to get manicky. One way I can tell is that I actually had fun, laughing and playing with my husband the other night and exulting in getting an old friend to walk straight into an awful joke. (**Me:** Have you heard the new Ebola joke going around. **Him:** No, what is it? **Me:** Eh, you probably won't get it. **Him:** No, c'mon, try me. **Me:** That WAS the joke. **Him** in evident pain: Oh! Oh! Oh! Oh! Oh! Oh!)

But the real clue that the upswing may be swinging more than it should: I'm thinking about starting more blogs. I already have two – this one and a general-purpose blog called Et Cetera, etc. (janetcobur.wordpress.com, if you're interested). I have met my goal of posting something in both of them once a week.

Then the big low hit me. But I'm back on track now, after several weeks' absence.

The thing is, I have ideas for two other blogs. I just don't know if I could handle them.

One would be Cats, Etc. – stories and anecdotes about life with cats, cat care and health, and so forth. We have three cats right now (Louise, Garcia, and Dushenka), plus many former fur-family members, so there would be no shortage of material.

The other idea is Books, Etc. I'm an avid reader, and though the bipolar has sapped my concentration so much that it varies between 20 minutes to two hours at a time, I'm starting to see some progress. And I find myself wanting to write about what I'm reading, maybe book reviews, maybe lists or quotations, maybe even some lit crit, my original background.

But could I maintain them? And not have them drain off the limited energy that I should use to do the freelance work that pays the bills.

I *think* it is a sign that I'm still fairly well anchored that I haven't rushed off and started them already. But the yearning to do more reading and writing keeps getting stronger. Maybe I could keep my current two at once a week and do the others on alternate weeks. But that would still mean three blog posts per week, plus the freelance. Frankly, I don't know if I could handle it. I keep asking myself, should I try? Or should I wait to see if my moods level out on the Abilify and it becomes clear whether they are Good or Bad Ideas, or even possible.

Words, both reading and writing them, have sustained me for most of my life. It was a sign of my most profound depression when I found myself unable to maintain enough focus to read. Now that I can again read and write to some extent, do I dare to push myself, push the boundaries? Can I? Should I?

Good thing I see my psychotherapist today.

The Fragility of Hypomania

I WAS IN IRELAND, on a bus full of journalists and two monsignors. The sun was shining, though the day was cool. We were on our way to some scenic inn where there would be a fragrant peat fire and servings of Irish coffee.

The guide was playing a mixtape through the bus's sound system. The song playing was "All God's Critters," by Bill Staines, a folk song I knew quite well. Here's the chorus:

> All God's critters got a place in the choir
> Some sing low, some sing higher
> Some sing out loud on the telephone wires
> And some just clap their hands, or paws, or anything they got now

I was happy, with that golden glow of joy I had felt so seldom in my life. I was peaceful, with a sense of everything being put in place especially, just for me. I was contented, beyond glad to be where I was and doing what I was doing.

Then one of the other people on the bus asked the guide to turn off the tape. It was weird, she said, and didn't make sense.

I don't know whether she didn't like folk music, or Bill Staines, or that song in particular. Perhaps she thought it was a children's song. Perhaps she thought we should be listening to something authentic and Irish.

But the guide turned off the tape. And my golden glow was gone. I was still on a bus in Ireland, traveling through sunshine toward a scenic little inn somewhere.

But my feeling of well-being was gone. It was like the breeze had blown it out through the windows of the bus. Everything became plain.

I didn't do anything about it at the time, ask to wait till the song was over or say it was one of my favorite songs, though now I like to think I would.

Was it hypomania that settled briefly on me like an aura? I hadn't been introduced to the concept then, but I think that's what it was. Peace, joy, well-being, a sense of being right where I fit. That could have been just regular happiness, I suppose. But it felt different, and special, and exhilarating.

And it was so fleeting. Once it was gone, it wouldn't come back. I enjoyed other parts of the trip, but never recaptured that singular moment, that uplifting rush.

Even a regular good mood is hard for me to hang onto. If someone around me is grumpy or cranky, I find it hard not to get sucked into the downward spiral. If they're *angry* forget it. There's no holding on to any good feeling then. My natural instinct is to cringe, and to apologize.

Or at least it was. As I have slowly gotten stronger and more stable, I do not cower the way I used to. I remove myself from the sucking drain of a person or situation if I can.

Going into the kitchen to make tea is a strategy I have often used. It's also a grounding method I can use when things are spinning out of control. When everything around me is chaos, the simple, familiar, soothing action of heating a pan of soup can bring me closer to stability. Whether I really want tea or soup is not the question. Making it for someone else may even be more calming.

Right now, I am pretty far from hypomania. I am fighting off two infections, plus the medications and debilitation that go with that. But at least now I know what hypomania feels like when it hits, and maybe I can hang onto it for just a little bit longer the next time.

Out of the House, At Last

IF EVERYTHING GOES according to plan, which we all know it never does, this post will be publishing itself while I am at or on my way to Brandywine Falls in Cuyahoga National Park.

I was attracted to this particular location when I read on the Internet that, in addition to access via a 1.75-mile hiking trail, the falls could also be reached using a wooden boardwalk from a nearby parking lot.

This easy access appeals to me because I have balance problems and sometimes use a cane, as well as because I seldom leave the house and have difficulty walking any distance. My husband encourages me to get out and walk, reminding me that exercise is good for depressive episodes, but just getting out of the house for doctors' appointments and a few errands leaves me with no spoons for recreational walking. It's a pretty dreary life, though there is a nice window in my study, through which I can see shrubs and trees, the occasional hummingbird or squirrel, or that stupid bird that sometimes flies straight into the glass and bonks itself silly.

There were actually tears in my eyes when I mentioned the expedition to Dan.

"What's the matter?" he asked.

"Would you drive a long way with me to do something that requires very little time to do?"

"What do you want to do?"

"See this waterfall," I said, pointing at the screen. I explained about the parking lot and the boardwalk.

"How far is it?"

"Near Cleveland. About three hours. Each way."

It sounded ridiculous even as I said it. A six-hour drive to walk a very short distance and look at a waterfall.

"We could stop along the way to get something to eat. Or we could pack a picnic. You could bring your camera and take nature photos."

I needn't have worked so hard to make it sound attractive. Getting out of the house to go see something scenic and outdoors is something my husband has been longing for us to share.

Naturally, as soon as we agreed to go, my brain went into overdrive, doing my usual job of trying to anticipate everything. We would need to Google Map directions, of course. We would need a waterproof bag with cold packs and bottles of water. Bandanas to moisten and wipe our sweaty brows (the temperature will likely be in the 80s and I don't do well in heat). Bug spray. My cane and maybe a walking stick for him. At times like this, I tend to plan the Normandy Invasion.

This is a ridiculous idea/plan. After the last month and a half I've had, it's a wonder that I'm not just crouched in a corner going beeble-beeble-beeble. But if it works, we may make the same drive in a few weeks to go to a horticultural center and canopy walk, if only so I can make the old, bad joke: You can lead a horticulture, but you can't make her think. We can meet up with some Cleveland-area friends we haven't seen in far too long.

So. Getting out. Exercise. Nature. Relaxation. Fresh air. No computer access. Potential socializing. I don't know whether these things will have any actual positive effects, but I like to think that my therapist will be proud of me.

Never mind that there are plenty of places locally to walk short distances and see nature. Never mind that my therapist often recommends that I take baby steps. This *is* a baby step. For God's sake, I used to be able to hike in the Adirondacks. To travel. To Europe. By myself.

I don't know why I was able to do that then but can't now. Bipolar disorder didn't strike me suddenly, after I had done all those things. Maybe back then I was better at functioning. Maybe life and bipolar had not yet overwhelmed my ability to cope. Maybe I was in remission, or whatever they call it. Maybe I was hypomanic. It's a mystery to me.

But maybe, just maybe, I can take this baby step toward reclaiming some of the things that used to bring me pleasure. It's about damn time.

I Got Away Successfully!

LAST WEEK I mentioned that my husband and I were planning a day trip to Cuyahoga National Park to see Brandywine Falls. This was based on a sudden, nearly inexplicable urge to get out of the house, get some fresh air, and see nature, despite my aversion to exercise. Maybe I was a little manicky. Who knows?

I'm happy to report that the trip was a success. The drive was long and hot, but that gave us plenty of time for conversation. We got lost a couple of times in the park area – it's a big, oddly shaped park. With a little help we found the right parking lot and even grabbed a space near the trailhead. As advertised, there was a boardwalk that led right to the falls, or at least to an overlook with a great view.

There were also 69 steps leading down to the falls, or, more to the point, 69 steps leading back up to the boardwalk and the overlook. I declined to attempt the stairs, but my husband did, and got some pretty good pictures.

Since it was Father's Day, there were a number of families there, but not so many that the trail seemed like a line for the rides at Disney World. The weather was ungodly hot, in the 90s as we were driving home, but the boardwalk was shady and there was a bit of a breeze.

So, what did I learn from this little adventure? First, that travel, at least on a small scale, is possible for me. I liked it so well that I am looking forward to taking another such trip, though most likely when the weather is cooler.

I drove the whole way up and back and was not bothered by my fears of drivers in the other lanes or railings and concrete dividers being too close to our car. This is a thing that used to happen, even when I was a passenger. Driving was out of the question back then.

Second, that I could make this trip with only minimal panic. I did have a moment on the way home. We stopped to eat, and as I rummaged in my bag for my regular glasses, I couldn't find them. I thought they were pretty likely to be in the car, though I had visions of the case lying on one of the benches along the boardwalk. I was even trying to figure out whom to call or write that might be in charge of lost and found.

However, I managed to suppress the feelings, read the menu with my sunglasses on (that actually may have been the hardest part), resist the urge to ask Dan to go out to the car and check, and get through the meal.

The glasses case proved to be in the car and I managed to avoid either panic or mini-meltdown. I call that success. I finished driving home, we fed the animals, and then collapsed. It was exhausting and exhilarating and adventurous and restorative, and most of all, proof that I could travel again, at least for a medium-short jaunt. Travel was one of my greatest joys and one of the things I've missed most since the bipolar stole so many parts of my life. I am delighted to be able to say that I am beginning to reclaim it.

Looking Back – But How Far?

"**LOOK AT WHERE** you are now compared to where you were when we started. Look how far you've come."

This is what my therapist frequently tells me. And she's right.

When I first came to see her, I was a total mess. It is a measure of my progress that I no longer refer to myself as "pathetic." it has been months, years, since I have used that word to describe myself.

And she is right to point out my progress. Not only am I no longer the despondent, distraught, weeping mess that came to her, I am now a person who has acquired coping skills, at least a few, that I can use in everyday life without much prompting from her.

But when I look back at how far I've come, how far back should I look?

Do I look back to my childhood, when there was something wrong with me that I didn't understand? Do I look back to the everyday traumas that a typical person would have dealt with, if not easily, then at least adequately, that often left me a crumpled figure in the corner weeping copiously and, yes, pathetic?

Since those days, I've learned what my disorder is, and have learned to anticipate and deal with some of those everyday traumas.

Do I look back to my teenage years, when I had little clue how to make and keep friends? When I was an outcast for my oddities?

Since then I have rediscovered old friends and made new ones that love and support me, many of whom are just as odd as I am.

Do I look back to my college days, when the bright promise of my intellect was dulled by my inner turmoil, when I missed out on opportunities because I was not capable of reaching out to grasp them?

Since then I have tried to make the most of opportunities that come my way, and to use my talents as best I can.

Do I look back to my first Significant Other and how that relationship shredded what I had managed to accumulate of self-esteem and confidence?

Since then I have been trying to recover as much as I can of what I lost. And I now have a stable, supportive, long-term relationship.

Do I look back to the days when I first lived independently, teetering on the edge of financial disaster? The days when I could barely function in the world of work and living, when the loss of a job put me deep in the Pit of Despair?

Since then, I have learned to accept help from others and to know that the Pit of Despair is not my permanent home.

Do I reflect on the job that sustained me for many years, until my emotional state became so fragile that I was no longer reliable enough to do it?

Since then I have gotten work that I can do reliably and found a niche for myself in the world of work.

Do I look back to that dreadful time when my brain broke, I became unable to work at all, unable to take care of myself, unable to function in anything like normalcy?

Since then, I have been rebuilding my life, not as good as new, but the best I can.

Admittedly, the distance I've come since then has been vast. I can't take the credit for it, however. Medications, therapy, a support system, a supportive husband, lots of reading about depression and anxiety and feminist issues and bipolar disorder have helped me survive and helped me grow.

Like many people with bipolar disorder I often have the sense that all along I was faking it, that during the periods when I seemed to be functioning best, I was pretending. Sometimes I think that's what I'm doing now.

What's that they say? Fake it till you make it?

But how do you know when you've made it?

I guess it's when you look back and remember, but no longer viscerally feel, what you went through. I still have unanswered questions, unresolved conflicts, and unanswered puzzles from all those former times.

I no longer think that I will get answers to all of them. I suppose their purpose now is simply to be mile markers, measuring the distance I have come. I can look back if I choose to, or not. I can look back at who and what I was, or as my therapist says, how far I've come. But I'm not pathetic anymore.

So, this is how far I've come. Can I look back without fear? Without despair? Sometimes I can. And that's not something I've always been able to say. It's progress.

Beware the Mental Health Meme!

This post was specially written for BlogHer's Social Media and Blogging section. (Credit for the photo goes to my husband, Dan Reily.)

Most Internet memes are harmless, or even amusing. They proclaim that someone has a wonderful granddaughter or that kittens are cute.

But some memes that travel the world sow unhelpful or even hurtful ideas as they go. The one above appears mild and even inspiring, but to a person with mental illness, it says a lot more than appears on the surface.

The meme that started me on this train of thought was one that invited people to embrace the crazy or enjoy the madness or some such. As a person with mental illness I found the message troubling. The comments were even more so. One said that manic-depressives could at least enjoy the mania.

Admittedly, mania comes with feelings of soaring confidence and a whirlwind of creativity. Mania can also prompt risky behaviors: reckless driving, shoplifting, unsafe and/or extramarital sex. All that can lead to a lifetime of problems, including failed relationships, arrest records, serious debt, and worse. Those are surely the opposite of enjoyable.

But I didn't know if I was alone in these feelings, so I asked other bipolar bloggers how they react to popular memes. Here's what they had to say.

Nondescript inspirational memes, of the sort that proclaim daylight follows darkness seem relatively harmless. Reactions went from "meh" to "a waste of time." Bipolar blogger Brad Shreve likens them to affirmations. His research showed that evidence from reputable studies confirms that affirmations mitigate stress. Nevertheless, "I find most of them trite and condescending," he says. "They just aren't my thing. I choose meditation."

Amy Balot, who blogs at madwomanacrossthewater.net, dislikes the sort of memes that tout positivity. "I do have a big problem with the way a lot of 'motivational' images seem to imply that all you need to do is think positive thoughts and your life will be hunky-dory," she says. "It seems to be blaming people for things like depression or anxiety."

Supposedly positive memes raise the hackles on a number of the bloggers. Dyane Leshin-Harwood, blogger at proudlybipolar.wordpress.com and author of the upcoming memoir *Birth of a New Brain*, says they range from "cool and empowering" to "[make] me feel guilty that my life isn't as good as it could be! It seems like it would bring anyone with bipolar depression down even further."

It does that to me as well.

Many such memes also promote a "bootstrap" approach to mental illness, which Jim Buchanan, who blogs at mythoughts62.wordpress.com, finds "irritating." "I feel that this sort of thinking is harmful, and it essentially blames the person reading it for their problems by implying that they 'don't want to allow themselves' what is needed for a good life."

Shreve adds, "Usually these entail [the idea that] the individual can change by doing one thing: [changing] our attitude. As if we could just snap out of depression, mania and more, if we would just put [our] mind to it. I find these guilty of mental health shaming."

And as for the "find-your-sanity-in nature" meme that began this article? Amy Balot doesn't care for that type. "I don't dispute that spending time with animals or outdoors can be great and even therapeutic; but I do dispute the implication that these things are a replacement for therapy or better than therapy," she says. "It minimizes the struggles of the mentally ill and says they'd be ok if they just took their dogs for more walks in the woods. Not all problems are solved by a little sunshine and fresh air."

Memes intended to be humorous are a gray area, since humor is so subjective. Personally, I don't mind being called "crazy," but many bipolar people do. Using "crazy," "insane," or any of the many synonyms such as "weird," "eccentric," or "not normal" can make people with mental disorders feel as if the meme speaks directly to them, even if that wasn't intended.

But some people with mental disorders enjoy a gentle poke of fun at themselves. Shreve agrees: "These can be touchy because they could hurt or offend someone who is going through a difficult time, but they help me."

I must admit that I can sometimes see humor in our situations. I've written humorous pieces. It's not a matter of malice being intended; I don't think people who pass along memes that we consider hurtful are "out to get" those with mental disorders. But that's the problem: They don't think before they click "Share."

So, I'm asking: Please think first. One of four Americans will have a mental or mood disorder at some time during their lives. You wouldn't make fun of someone with a physical illness. Ask yourself: Would this meme still be amusing or inspiring or helpful if you substituted fibromyalgia or diabetes or paraplegia for "mental illness"?

If not, think again.

Chapter Seven: On the Upside

Cookie Theory • Misery and Math • Confessions of a Crazy Cat Lady • Work Hacks • In Defense of the Armadillo • Bipolar Me vs. Disney World • Those Science Fiction Crazies • The Depression Diet • Brain vs. Brain

Cookie Theory

MANY OF YOU are probably already familiar with Spoon Theory.

Just as I didn't invent Spoon Theory, I can't claim Cookie Theory as my own. My husband shared it with me, on the weekend over 30 years ago when we met.

I was having a difficult time (to say the least) with my boyfriend at the time, whom we'll call Rex. Among the difficulties was that I was stranded, several hundred miles from home, with no money. I had to borrow from every single person I knew there, including some, like my future husband, that I had just met, in order to get bus fare. And find someone who would take me to the bus station.

Dan, the aforementioned future husband, was the one who gave me a ride, and as I was waiting for the bus, he shared with me these words of wisdom:

Just because someone hands you shit cookies doesn't mean you have to eat them.

The more I pondered this metaphor, the more I realized how insightful it was. Rex had generously supplied me with shit cookies over the year and a half I knew him. And I ate them. I was also supposed to pretend they were chocolate chip. And say yum, yum.

And I did.

The bus wasn't the only thing that stopped for me that day. So did my willingness to eat the cookies.

The first step is training yourself to recognize the difference between shit cookies and chocolate chip. The second is saying no. Like refusing an invitation to an argument. Just say no and walk away. Or catch a bus.

I'm not claiming it's easy. But when someone hands you a put-down, a micro-aggression, a lie, ask yourself, "Is this a chocolate chip cookie?"

If not, don't take it. Don't eat it.

Then stay on that diet. It's amazing how much weight it will take off you.

Misery and Math

ONE DAY, WHEN I had too much time on my hands, I came up with a theory: The Mathematics of Misery.

Basically, there are two stages of misery: wallowing and getting over it.

In my theory, the wallowing stage is necessary. You need to feel the misery, own the feeling, and try to figure out what, if anything, caused it. If you omit this stage, you won't learn whatever lesson there is.

Then you move on to the getting over it stage. Ideally, the getting over it should involve eliminating the cause of the misery, keeping in mind that there are laws against homicide.

Now, here comes the mathematics.

According to my theory, the proper proportion should be 20 percent wallowing and 80 percent getting over it. But for me, that's an unreachable goal, especially before I was medicated. Thirty to 35 percent wallowing is more realistic. It's when the scale tips over 50 percent wallowing that you need to get help. Preferably professional help. And I've been *way* over that tipping point.

It's like the stupid scale in the doctor's office. I just keep trying to slide the weight closer to the getting over it end.

Confessions of a Crazy Cat Lady

ONE CAN BE a crazy cat lady without living alone in a cavernous house with a dozen or more cats. I should know. I don't and I am one.

First let's start with definitions. I'm crazy. I think we all know that by now and I don't mind saying so. I'm also a cat lady. We had dogs growing up, but I never got very close with them. I did have a rabbit that I was awfully fond of, but this was in the days before lop-eared rabbits became house pets. She lived in a cage in the garage, or in the back yard when the weather was nice.

To me a crazy cat lady is someone who has eight or more cats, lives alone with them, usually in a large house, but one not quite big enough for all the inhabitants. Often you hear news stories about crazy cat ladies who die alone and are eaten by their cats, or crazy cat ladies whose pets are taken away from them because of inadequate care, especially sanitation.

I have a friend who has had more than eight cats at once, and is just as crazy as I am. She does *not*, however, believe that she is a crazy cat lady because another lady down the street has *more* cats. And truthfully, she doesn't meet the other requirements of crazy-cat-lady-hood. She has a family and keeps up with the care and feeding of her menagerie.

Do crazy cat ladies have an actual mental disorder? If so, do they all have the same kind? Maybe not. The crazy cat lady on *The Simpsons* (Eleanor Abernathy) is clearly schizophrenic, though I doubt that many are in real life. Real-life cat ladies may demonstrate obsessive-compulsive tendencies, or their isolation may be due to depression. Or something else entirely.

Psychology Today tells us there is no real basis for the stereotype. "The stereotypic term 'crazy cat lady' is used in a pejorative sense to classify an older, female animal hoarder and there is no research to support such correlation. Research on animal hoarding is lacking and there is not one plausible theory that suggests why older females tend to hoard animals more than men."

Still, crazy cat lady behavior may be psychologically classified as a "hoarding disorder." *Mother Nature Network* reports that the condition "is only now getting the recognition that will prove helpful to sufferers. Recent research has revealed abnormal brain activity in people with hoarding disorder." And both experts and hoarders hope and believe that the new DSM classification will help bring about better treatment.

I would make the case that crazy-cat-lady-hood is actually a *defense* against mental disorders. Carried to an extreme, perhaps, but beneficial nonetheless.

Caring for cats gives a person another living being to care about. Patients in geriatric facilities are often brought into contact with small, domesticated farm animals or cats and dogs, which pretty clearly help them deal with isolation and depression.

For an isolated person, cats provide someone to talk to. Not that the cats necessarily listen or respond, of course, except in the most perverse ways possible. They are cats, after all.

I got my first cat when I was living alone and recovering from several years of psychological trauma. My future husband went with me to the shelter, but was studiously unhelpful in selecting a cat, thereby proving that he had some sense and a grasp of how important it was for me to find a kitty I could bond with.

"Which one should I get?" I asked.

"Gee," he replied, "I dunno, honey. They all look like nice cats to me."

The one I chose was Bijou, a tortoiseshell.

We as a couple have since had up to five cats at a time, and through the years a total of well over a dozen.

When my bipolar disorder was at its worst, after I had suffered a major meltdown (nervous breakdown, decompensation, or whatever you call it), I was certainly crazy, but hardly a cat lady. I was unable to take care of my own daily needs, much less those of anyone else, human or feline. My husband, who was taking up enormous amounts of slack, took over pet care as well. Now that I'm back on a fairly even keel, I can do my part with feeding, litter box tending, grooming, and so forth.

Fortunately, even when I was immobilized, my cats, in addition to my husband, gave me emotional sustenance. The therapeutic effects of a purr, a gentle kneading, and a nice snuggle are not to be underestimated. The antics of a kitten may be exhausting to watch, but they provide more than a little distraction.

Do dogs have the same therapeutic effect? I don't know. For some people I suppose they do, but I have never bonded with a dog as I have with my cats.

In psychological terms, my cats are "comfort objects," like furry, living security blankets, or teddy bears that shit and meow. I hope never to be without a cat again. I need them for my mental health.

Work Hacks

YAY ME! I just finished the first phase of a big project for which I will be paid actual money!

I am very fortunate/grateful that I am able to do freelance work at home, on my own schedule (mostly), using my education and skills, in my pajamas. Telecommuting is so way cool!

I can't work an eight-hour day in an office any more, and likely won't again. I can only concentrate for a max of three hours at a time, and some days not even that. Occasionally, if there's a tight deadline, I can manage two sessions, or one and a half.

Of course, motivation is a factor. Deadlines and money are two really good ones. But sometimes I have to force myself, or trick myself into doing actual work. This was true even when I did work in an office.

Anyway, here are some of my techniques.

Taking breaks. Now of course, I can take breaks whenever I want, from a quick game of Candy Crush to an actual nap. My brain and body let me know when it's time. They just crap out.

When I worked at the office, I tried taking crossword puzzle breaks at my desk. But apparently smoking was the only permissible break activity. Hiding in the bathroom didn't work either. People were known to track me down and ask questions anyway. "Do you mind if I wipe and flush first?" Sarcasm seemed called for.

When I got twitchy, I walked around the third floor or even more than one floor until I calmed down. The trick is to carry a clipboard or a few manila folders and walk sort of briskly, so it looks like you're going somewhere and doing something. It works best if the office has more than one room.

Pretending to work. I developed this technique at the office, but it can also be used at home. I would say to myself, "I don't know how to get started. I'll just write one sentence, so if someone walks by my cube, it looks like I'm working." It was surprising to find that once the first sentence was on the screen, I knew what the second one should be, or that if the first one was horrible, I could revise it, which also looked like work. Once I built some momentum this way, I was rolling. I don't have anyone looking over my shoulder now, but the idea is the same: one sentence is the minimum, then see what happens.

Bribery and rewards. These are actually more or less the same. If I do X amount of work, I can check my email or eat a cookie or call a friend. I get to feel virtuous for working and satisfied by the little treat.

Forcing myself. If I've got a really tight deadline, I have to apply some internal pressure, especially if it's one of those I-don't-think-I-can-get-out-of-bed days. Everyone in this house likes to eat. The cats insist on it. My pay will cover the mortgage, so we won't be living under the Third St. Bridge next month. This is dangerous, because I am a great catastrophizer, but sometimes it's the only thing that works.

Artificial goals and lying to myself. If I can just do five more pages I can quit for the day. I know I can make it to the end of this section (that would be the lying part).

Stupid work. There are a lot of fairly pointless tasks that must be done anyway but can be done by rote: adding headers and footers and page numbers, alphabetizing, running spell-check or typing-check, as I prefer to think of it. That sort of thing. To me, that counts as actual work, and some days it's all I can manage.

Unfortunately, none of these are effective for housework. No one pays me for that.

In Defense of the Armadillo

LET'S CONSIDER the armadillo.

I have always identified with the armadillo, for a variety of reasons. It is the symbol of Texas music, which I love. I have a purse shaped like an armadillo. I also have toy armadillos, crocheted armadillos, wooden, stone, cement, armadillo jewelry, you name it. My uncle and I have a catch-phrase: *El armadillo amarillo de mi tía es sobre la mesa.*

What does all this have to do with bipolar disorder? I'm glad you asked.

Most of all, I admire the armadillo for its defense mechanisms, which resemble some of mine.

The armadillo has armor (obviously). I have tried to construct a similar impervious shell. When I have been even partially successful, it has proved counterproductive. When you wall off feelings, you wall off the good ones too.

The armadillo rolls up in a tight ball. I isolate. This has also proved counterproductive. If sorrow shared is halved and joy shared is doubled, then isolation, well, you do the math.

The armadillo leaps vertically when threatened. My anxiety makes me jump and release fight-or-flight hormones. This defense is also counterproductive, both for the armadillo and for me. One of the armadillo's main predators is the automobile; the armadillo jumps straight up to bumper height. I waste energy on panicky behaviors even when I'm not threatened.

The armadillo has a low body temperature and is therefore useful for research on leprosy. This is not a defense mechanism, but it *is* a Fun Fact to Know and Tell. I have never had leprosy.

All things considered, the armadillo is not a good role model for a person (me) with bipolar disorder. But I like them anyway. They remind me that I need to check whether my defenses are doing me harm rather than good.

Plus, with my armadillo handbag I get lots of practice in the social skill of making light conversation with strangers, even children!

Bipolar Me vs. Disney World

ONCE A GROUP of us were on a business trip to Anaheim. "If any of you want to take clients to Disneyland, I can get you tickets," the boss said.

"I can't even imagine myself wanting to do that," I replied.

The others laughed, though I wasn't trying to be funny. I get that a lot.

I have always had deeply mixed feelings about Walt Disney and his creations. How could I not? A place that bills itself as The Happiest Place on Earth vs. Bipolar 2 That Has Caused Depression since Childhood. To be fair, I used to like "Wonderful World of Color," particularly the nature films, even when we had only a B&W TV. Gray Tinkerbelle is a metaphor for. . . well, something involving depression.

So, what explains this picture of a dear friend, me, and my husband being photo-bombed by a Lego dragon?

The first thing you have to know about Tom (left) and Leslie (the photographer) is that their inner children are, let's say, very close to the surface. They are Disney World aficionados. And they know all (well, almost all) about my mental disorders.

We desperately needed a vacation, and they offered to be our guides for an adult-friendly, non-teacup visit. Also, it was the Millennium celebration and early in December, which promised no sweltering heat, interesting decorations, and other spiffy stuff, including few children, who would not yet be on Christmas break.

Here's what I learned.

- The restaurants there are incredible. Eat your way around Epcot.
- I dreaded the Tower of Terror because I thought my stomach would drop out. This proved not to be the problem; my inner ear objected, though. Our friends got me on it by telling me to repeat the mantra, "Disney will not kill me. They want more of my money later." It was one of those Things That I'm Glad I Did and Now Will Never Do Again.
- The Explorer's Club is extremely cool.
- There are lots of nifty tiny things that aren't rides and attraction that you can try to spot – bits of the sidewalk that light up randomly like a surprise Dance Dance Revolution, Mickey Mouse ear shapes in unexpected places, such as the wing nuts on shelves in the many gift shops, and so on. This is where knowledgeable guides come in particularly handy.
- At night, you can see the stars from the top of that mining train-roller coaster thing, something I didn't expect, given all the ambient light an amusement park puts out.

- Also, we all won giant purple-and-red plush armadillos at one of the games. That's one thing *my* inner child can appreciate.
- STAY AWAY from the teacups and It's a Small World. They will turn you into a whimpering, burbling puddle of regret and sugar-shock. When your mother asks later, just say, "Oh, yes. They were nice. You would have loved them."

If you go with the right people, do not try to make it into the Bataan Fun March, and rest and eat or retreat to the hotel when you need a break. It's survivable and even (dare I say it?) enjoyable. Sufficiently medicated with Prozac and Ativan, I could handle it.

I'd have to give this round to Disney, but really it was all Tom and Leslie.

P.S. Also, the Food and Wine Festival is a great experience. I spent three months in Orlando and a co-worker got us tickets. Cute guys with devastating Australian accents chatting about Australian wine. What could possibly be more satisfactory?

Those Science Fiction Crazies

THERE HAS RECENTLY been a huge kerfuffle in the science fiction community regarding the Hugo Awards. You don't really need to know much about it and probably don't want to. Suffice it to say that two groups had it out over the past and future direction of science fiction and fantasy, and the meaning of the asterisk.

The awards have now been given, but still the blogosphere is full of recriminations, sour grapes, and schadenfreude.

What does this have to do with mental health? Aside from the fact that very smart people can behave like vicious toddlers, it's interesting to note that the various sides in this dispute did not always, shall we say, act rationally. You probably guessed that from the asterisks.

This phenomenon is not unique to the Hugo Awards. If you have never been to a science fiction convention, let me tell you about it.

Most of the people there will be very intelligent, obsessive about their fields of interest, lacking in social skills to various degrees, and will have a history of being outcast or bullied in their youth.

Does any of that sound familiar?

I'm not a psychologist, nor do I play one on TV, but I can't help thinking that if you tested everyone at one of these events they would score higher than a random group of people on the autism spectrum. Simply put, the SF community appears to have more than its share of Aspies, and a fair sprinkling of bipolar, depressive, and OCD people.

When their oddities are carried to the extreme, and they often are, SF fandom can devolve into incivility that results in unconscionable threats and exceedingly ugly online behavior.

When you see these kinds of behavior, it is tempting to dismiss science fiction fans as being the caricatures that the media have instilled in us: clueless losers who live in their parents' basements, show up at jury duty dressed in Star Trek uniforms, and insist that Harry should have ended up with Hermione.

Admittedly, to a certain extent that is true. If you look around at a convention you will almost certainly see a number of people who conform to that stereotype. I myself have a relative who could be Queen of the Get-a-Lifes.

What you may not see is that, despite the cluelessness, rudeness, sometimes elitist or misogynistic behavior, obsessiveness, and disregard for the feelings of others, the science fiction community is, at heart, a place where the non-typical person can find a group of like-minded individuals to talk with, obsess with, bond with, and occasionally practice social skills with. It fulfills a very real social and psychological need. Without the science fiction community, whether online or in "meatspace," many of these people would have little or even no place to have much of a social life at all.

Certainly, the stereotype is not true of all members of fandom. Most hold regular jobs in technical, creative, or other fields; have families and close relationships; and negotiate their way through modern society as well or poorly as anyone else. But there are consistencies in their backgrounds. Most are incessant readers and have been since childhood. Many have been the targets of cliques in school and the workplace. A number would be described by their neighbors as quiet loners, though this is not to imply that SF fandom harbors more spree killers than any other group. They have odd senses of humor or in some cases none at all. In a very real sense, sf fandom is for them, as one song would have it, made up of "My Thousand Closest Friends."

So, if you happen to be in a hotel and find the meeting space is overflowing with people dressed as Klingons, robots, and giant furry animals, remember that they are mostly harmless and enjoying a moment of fitting in to a part of society that celebrates and honors their differences and shares their pride in their oddness. Where they can relax and be themselves, without worrying about seeming weird or threatening or being put down, avoided, or scorned. Think of it as a support group with parties, art shows, panel discussions, music, costumes, movies, and chocolate.

A lot of us with mental disorders are glad to know that such places exist. A lot of us wish we could find or make such places, too.

The Depression Diet

IT SEEMS THAT stores can now send, well, targeted ads based on previous purchases. The example usually given is that someone who buys a home pregnancy test will start receiving coupons and discount offers on diapers and strollers.

I maintain that one way to spot depressives is through their grocery-buying habits. Just as psychologists say that odds are that the last three people in any long line are likely to be clinically depressed, I say that someone who purchases an entire chocolate chip cheesecake and a bottle of Jose Cuervo is going to be in the back of that check-out line, too.

Which brings me to my point. There are certain foods that depressed people tend to eat. These foods don't cure depression, of course, but they do seem to provide some comfort.

The first category of depression food is, of course, comfort food. We all have our own definitions of comfort food, but a lot of them seem to be high-carb, high-fat, no-nutrition sorts of food. They bring back memories of childhood, maternal nurturing, and a simpler time when calories didn't count. Some of my comfort foods include club sandwiches, grilled cheese with tomato soup, mashed potatoes, and macaroni and cheese.

My husband knows enough to make me comfort food when I'm stressed out. He does add tuna fish and peas to the mac and cheese to make it somewhat more nutritious. He knows my needs and does well at meeting them, though his grilled cheese will never rival my mother's. He does pretty well on the tomato soup.

The next category of depression food is weird food. I suppose this category includes the chocolate chip cheesecake and tequila. One of my depressed friends introduced me to her particular specialty: wavy potato chips dipped in cream cheese with an M&M stuck on top. My husband starts to worry about me if I ask him to pick these up for me at the store. But it does contain all four food groups: salty, sticky, sweet, and crunchy.

When I was a kid, my favorite was a block of cream cheese with that odd, unnaturally orange French dressing poured over it, mashed with a fork, and with pickle relish if I we had any. This was my own chip dip creation. It resembled my friend's in the cream cheese and wavy chips department, but French dressing is no substitute for M&Ms. Let's just say my tastes have grown, not necessarily up.

Another category of depression food is useless people food. These are edibles that one can make with very little effort, as even small efforts can be overwhelming at this point in depression. Frozen dinners are good for this. I recommend Marie Callender pot pies if you go this route, because they have both a top and bottom crust and so feel more like a meal. Foods that come in small cups with pop-open tops are good too: Beefaroni, mac and cheese, soups.

Sometimes, however, the depression is so severe that even these simple efforts are beyond you. For those occasions, there are truly useless foods. It's a mistake to call them meals at all. Here I'm talking peanut butter straight out of the jar (spoon optional), and dry cereal straight out of the box. During my worst days I used to keep a box of Cocoa Puffs by my bedside, just in case. As I slowly improved, I replaced that with a box of Life cereal. The name was a coincidence, I assure you.

I know that eating a well-balanced, nutritious diet is one of the most common suggestions for keeping depression at bay, along with exercise, sleep, and all that other good advice. I also remember that when a person is talking about suicide, one of the questions you're supposed to ask is, "When's the last time you ate?" Supposedly it's harder to take your own life if you've recently done something as life-affirming as eating. I don't know if that's actually true, but I did try it once and the person is still alive, so maybe.

I also know that sometimes irrational thinking extends to food choices as well. I worry about my husband when he starts eating peanut butter sandwiches dipped in cold, chunky, still-in-the-can soup . I've been told that's a guy thing, not a depressive thing, but still sometimes I wonder. Even at my most depressed, I've never been tempted to do that. Ew. Just ew.

Brain vs. Brain

HAVING BIPOLAR disorder is like having cognitive dissonance all the time.

What is cognitive dissonance? When people ask, I usually describe it as when the two halves of your brain slam forcefully into each other and give you a brain-ache. It's also known as "brain go 'splodey."

Take, for instance, the time when I saw excerpts from the musical *Cabaret*, performed by women, the very youngest of whom was at least 65. As I reeled out of the theater, my mother saw the dazed look on my face and said, "Don't you like *Cabaret*?"

"I *love Cabaret*!" I replied. Meanwhile, the other side of my brain was saying, "Oh my God, if they had tried to do the Bob Fosse choreography, someone would have broken a hip for sure!" Slam! Pow! 'Splodey! Cognitive dissonance.

You can probably see how this relates to bipolar. One half of your brain says, "If you just take a shower, you can go out to lunch." The other half says, "A shower?!? First, I have to find a clean towel and a bar of soap, get undressed without seeing myself in the mirror, fiddle with the water temperature, wash and shampoo, dry off, find clean underwear, and that's not even thinking about drying my hair and figuring out what I can wear! Oh, my God, I've used up all my spoons just thinking about it! I should just eat Cocoa Puffs and go back to bed."

Instant cognitive dissonance.

Or try this scenario: You see on your newsfeed that the government is considering a new law with a feel-good title regarding mental health issues. "Hooray!" you think. "At last! Everyone should support this fabulous bill!" Then you look at the whole article and find that one provision in the bill allows violating the privacy protections of HIPAA, as an example.

"Oh no!" the other half of your brain says. "Any person, even one who's mentally ill, has the right to medical privacy. What if an abuser gets information about his victim? I've got to write a letter protesting this bill. Where are my spoons? *Did someone steal my spoons?*"

There are lots of these situations, hence the near-permanent state of cognitive dissonance.

I want to be around people, but I don't want to talk to anyone.

I want to be left alone but then I'm lonely.

I really want to make love to my partner, but I can't get aroused.

I want to be cured but I hate the idea of being "normal."

That degree of cognitive dissonance is positively exhausting. No wonder we never want to do anything but lie in bed, not read, not interact, not reach out, not try to do anything but survive another day.

If we think too hard about anything, our brains may go 'splodey.

Chapter 8: The Social Whirl

A Closet of Disguises • Surviving High School (And Reunions) • How I Learned a Few Socials Skills • I Have This Friend . . . • I'm Not Brave – I'm Stubborn • Social but Spoonless • I May Have Miscounted My Spoons • A Crowd-Hater at a Conference • The Therapeutic Hug

A Closet of Disguises

I HAVE A business meeting to go to this week, and as it nears, my anxiety is building.

This used to be a thing I did all the time. I used to go to business conventions and work the booth and have business lunches and dinners and meet and greet and travel and wear suits and pantyhose and give speeches.

But that was quite a few years ago. Before my brain broke this last time. Since then I have worked at home when I'm able to, in front of my computer, in my pajamas. Now I have to remember how to do the other thing.

It's not even what I would call a really intimidating function. 45-minute drive. Four hours long. Biz cazh. (I think. I hope.) Billable. Free lunch, maybe someplace nice.

However. I want to look and act sane and articulate and relatively socially skillful. That could be an uphill climb. And it's been icy lately. Literally as well as figuratively.

A long time back I heard of a technique of imagining you had a closet of disguises for all the things you needed to be. When you needed them, you could reach into the closet and take out your Respectable Married Lady disguise or your Sophisticated World Traveler disguise or your Competent Business Woman disguise and put it on. Sometimes literally as well as figuratively.

But I fear the Competent Business Woman outfit is in tatters, eaten by moths, and hopelessly outdated. I'm not sure it will even fit.

So, I have to do the best I can in cobbling together a literal disguise, in hopes that it will trigger the figurative one. I will get my hair done (even though I can't afford it). I will try to pull together a decent casual outfit (nice jeans and a nice sweater and ballet flats?) instead of my usual look, which I invented and call Vintage Boho Hobo. I will see if I still have a coat that fits that isn't someone's cast-off army jacket. I will borrow my husband's car because mine had a flat and is still making do with the rubber doughnut spare. I will renew my driver's license. I will put some Ativan in my purse (do I still have one that isn't shaped like an armadillo?). Probably some Lomotil or Imodium too, in case I need to placate my irritable bowel. And several kinds of breath mints. Perhaps I should take my cane, so my balance problems don't make me look like a first-time ice skater or land me on my ass or all fours. And OMG, what can I do about make-up? I always stab myself in the eye with a mascara wand, so that's out. I'm sure that any make-up I have has expired and I really don't want to spend the money on new after the hair expense.

All this to get through four hours out in public meeting people other than teens behind the drive-through windows. I don't even want to look glamorous. Just not hopeless. Or homeless.

I would really rather Skype, since then I would just have to do the hair and the top half of an outfit.

I'm afraid that by the time I pull myself together, I'll be too tired to go.

Surviving High School (And Reunions)

I'VE ONLY EVER gone to one of my high school reunions, the 25th. Now the 40th is nearly here.

I was terrified then. This time is not as bad. I don't have the energy or the attention span to get all worked up about it. Will I go? Probably not. It's like the Tower of Terror at Disney World: I did it once and I'm glad I did, but I have no desire to do it again.

My difficulties with the 25th reunion even made the local paper. I went to a high school friend, Mary, for advice. She was quite helpful. She also, with my permission, wrote about my panic in her newspaper column.

Here's what I told her: "Over the last quarter century I've confronted and dealt with a number of pieces of my past and tried to make my peace with them. High school, however, is not one of those things. I'm afraid I'll have flashbacks."

Mary did note that I "... had more reason than most to be apprehensive. While I had been actively ignored, she had been, at times, actively picked on, one of those kids too brainy, too head-in-the-clouds, to comprehend how to navigate the social firmament."

Pretty close. Except that I wouldn't have called it "actively picked on." High school was merely another part of the continuum of bullying and harassment that I experienced from childhood on. In high school no one threw literal rocks at me, but by then they didn't have to. I was conditioned to cringe.

The head-in-the-clouds part was also not entirely accurate. As I walked through the halls between classes, my head was down, and my nose was in a book. I was trying to perfect my "invisible" act and practice that advice that the bullied always get, "just ignore them."

And I wouldn't call the social milieu in high school "the firmament." Just sayin'.

I did go to the reunion, though. I got my hair done for the event and told my stylist to make me look "successful and sane."

She replied, "Oh, no, here comes the wish list."

"At least I didn't ask for young and thin," I pointed out.

I went, taking along my husband and telling him not to leave my side. I'm sure the husband came as a surprise to most people there, proof that I had at least managed to navigate that particular social firmament. And if my hairstyle did proclaim some degree of sanity, that was likely a surprise as well.

I survived. My big insight: "Not everyone hated me." I should have known that already, since I had friends like Mary and a few others I'm still in touch with. But old fears die hard.

Mary was much more philosophical: "In adolescence our images are refracted through so many distorted lights: the way we see ourselves, the way everyone else sees us, the way we fancy everyone else sees us. What mattered was that we could all talk face to face, as adults, as equals, as friends."

She may have been right, though "Not everyone hated me" was, in its way, a major alteration in my outlook and pretty much as far as I'd gotten by then in my continuing struggle to come to grips with my life.

Things have changed a lot since high school and so have I. Now I realize I have nothing to prove and no need to try.

How I Learned a Few Social Skills

I THOUGHT MY social skills were bad until I encountered a woman who asked me, "Do you have mental problems?" She recognized me from our mutual psychiatrist's waiting room, but still....

With practice, however, I have been able to improve my casual conversation skills, at least enough to get by in some situations, as long as they don't last more than an hour. Here are my secrets. They do take practice. I have been fortunate to have had people to practice with – friends, coworkers, and of course my husband.

Introductions. Actually, I taught this one to my husband. Often when we met someone that he knew, he would fail to introduce me, leaving me standing there like the proverbial bump on a log. He claimed that the problem was that usually he couldn't remember the person's name. "Just point to me and say, 'This is my wife, Janet.' Then I will stick out my hand to shake and say, 'And you are?' That way we both learn the person's name." It works like a charm, every time.

Very Brief Conversations. Conversation with strangers, just a sentence or two, is also relatively easy to learn. The trick is the innocuous comment and there are two ways to go about it. The first is to make the comment yourself. "Those are great shoes! They make your feet look really small." "What a lovely handbag. My mother had one that was similar." Make an observation and then a related remark, usually complimentary. They don't even have to be true technically. If you can't think of anything else to say, a comment on the color of an outfit is usually good. There's hardly any way someone can take offense at "That's a great shade of blue on you."

The other side of the equation is to get someone else to make a comment to you. This requires a prop most of the time. I used to carry a purse shaped like an armadillo, and that proved a great conversation starter. I memorized several responses that I could use when the other person said, "Oh, what an unusual purse!" I could say, "My mother gave it to me for Christmas one year" or "A friend found it in some catalog." The purse went over big, especially if there were children present.

Longer Conversations. These require more practice. Luckily at one of the jobs I had, there were a couple of people that I could invite out to lunch and practice conversation with. I suspect that they knew what I was doing, but they never mentioned it. In effect, they played along. Mary, for example, had two adopted children, and questions about them were always good for a few minutes of interesting listening. Her family also had a cat and a snake. Pets and children make good topics.

Sometimes it's best to steer clear of work-related subjects, but if the person is really understanding, you may be able to vent. You should also be able to listen to the other person. The secret to that is not to try to fix the problem. Simply listen and validate the person's feelings. "That sounds awful! Does she do that all the time?"

Formal Settings. My coworker also provided me with the opportunity to learn about a sometimes-necessary but difficult situation: funerals. Mary and a few other people invited me to go with them to the viewing of a person that I knew only slightly in a work context, so the stakes were low. From watching Mary and her friends I learned that the proper procedure is to stand briefly at the coffin looking solemn, then go to the bereaved, shake hands or hug depending on whether they proffer a hand or two arms, and say, "I'm sorry for your loss" or "My deepest sympathy" and at least one remark about the departed. It can be as simple as "He was a pleasure to work with" or "Everyone at work is going to miss her."

Not Melting Down. Another important social skill is not having a major meltdown in front of other people. When I first visited my husband's family, I became very uncomfortable quite often because everyone seemed to be yelling at each other. Loud, angry voices tend to upset me, especially if they continue for any length of time. The technique I developed was to go into the other room and make a cup of tea. Making tea is socially acceptable. If you're in the kitchen, go to the bathroom or step outside for fresh air.

Much later I learned that my husband didn't realize that his family reacted to even minor questions with argumentative responses in loud voices. To him, and to them, this was simply the normal style of conversation. It wasn't what was normal in my family, and it triggered my aversion to confrontation. I guess whatever you grow up with seems normal to you.

One other piece of advice: Don't attempt flirting unless you have a coach. It's really tricky and possibly dangerous. Not for the novice, especially not the kind of novice who wears a habit.

I Have This Friend . . .

TO HAVE A FRIEND, be a friend.

That's how the saying goes, and it goes double for friends with mental disorders.

But.

There are limits. Boundaries. You may call them self-serving or self-saving, but there they are.

When you are depressed, you neglect friends, and I have certainly done that. I permanently lost at least one friend over it. But another kept reaching out to me and I eventually responded. We then had a good game of "I'm a bad friend." "No, I'm a bad friend." She thought she hadn't reached out often enough. I was glad she put up with my silence as long as she did, until I was able to reach back.

But I have this friend. We used to be tight. When we were both depressed, we shared our misery and so lessened it. But now that the Pit of Despair is no longer my permanent abode...I have to limit my contact.

Why? My social skills have never been terrific, but now I frequently find myself walking that invisible line between Bad Friend and burnout.

Why is it so hard to be a Good Friend?

First, there is the Disaster Report. Whenever I talk to her, I hear a litany of all that is going wrong in her life. Almost never anything else. I'm no fan of relentless positivity, but its opposite is sometimes hard to bear too, even though I've been guilty of the same.

Then there is the fact that any suggestions are pushed away, denied as impossible, dismissed as unworkable. Granted, we have completely different styles of coping, but I feel discounted, unheard. Eventually I gave up sharing anything but a few of my own tribulations, some awful jokes, and commiseration.

Then I get off the phone or off Facebook, usually after half an hour or so. That's about my limit.

I keep reaching out. I don't want to be a Bad Friend. I know I can't fix her, or even her day-to-day difficulties, the kind even non-depressed people have. But I sure wish there was a way I could help, short of climbing down into the Pit with her. I hope that listening, even half an hour at a time, does some good.

And when I talk to other friends of mine, I try to remember to ask how their day was and what's new in their life and have they seen any good movies and what is a mutual friend doing. I try to listen if they have something to share, good or bad, and I try not to overwhelm them or play whose-life-sucks-the-most. I try to be a Not-Bad Friend, even if I do have to lean on my friends, at times pretty heavily.

And they do likewise, when they can.

I'm Not Brave – I'm Stubborn

ONE OF MY FRIENDS, who is overweight, recently told me that when she was at the gym on the treadmill, a stranger came over to her and told her she was "an inspiration."

My friend felt insulted. She was working out for herself and for her health, not to inspire anyone else or to be taken as a symbol of I-don't-know-what. Perseverance? Attitude? Effort? Hope?

I feel sort of the same way when people say that because I am open and public about my bipolar disorder that I am "brave."

I'm not doing this because I'm brave. I'm doing it because I'm stubborn.

I am who and what I am, and I'm willing to reveal a lot of it because, frankly, I can't hide it and don't want to. I'm not average or typical. Not normal, mentally or emotionally.

I've always had a love-hate relationship with the concept of "normal." Desperately wanting to appear normal but knowing viscerally that I am not. Wondering what it's like but knowing that I'll never know. Wondering what it even means, or what it means that I'm not. I haven't found answers yet, and at this point I don't think I'm going to. It's probably a waste of my time to try.

So, if I'm outside the "norm," which I am, I may as well admit it. And since writing is what I do, I write about it. I'm not doing this because I'm "brave," I'm doing this because on some level I have to. I'm stubborn.

I'm stubborn enough these days to have made a sort of peace with the concept of "normal," even though I still don't understand it.

I'm stubborn enough to acknowledge my difference and give it its proper name: bipolar disorder.

I'm stubborn enough not to care when I say that and some people flinch or back away.

I'm stubborn enough to reveal things that embarrass me because they are part of me and part of what I've lived and lived through.

I'm stubborn enough to get tattoos proclaiming my status as "mentally ill" and using them to open conversations and educate others.

I have not come to embrace my stubbornness easily. I've tried to fake "normal" and hide my differences. I've gone to my shrink and just referred to "doctor appointments." I've made Prozac jokes even though I was taking it at the time. For this I am truly sorry, as I later learned that one of those jokes made another person afraid to admit that she took Prozac too.

I'm not trying to be an "inspiration." I'm not trying to prove anything to anyone else. I'm doing what I have to do for me. If someone else finds some good in it, that's fine. But that's not why I do it.

I am bipolar.

I am a writer.

I am stubborn.

Taken together, you get this blog.

Bipolar Me.

Social But Spoonless

IN THE PAST WEEK I have been out of the house more and seen more people than I have in years. It's almost like having a social life.

In the past week I have also slept more than I usually do in my sloth-like, torpid existence.

I think the two are not unrelated.

The dry run for my recent spurt of socializing began last week. After I went for my final session with my doctor, I managed a trip to the bank, a trip to the place where I could pay my power bill, and since it was right next door, a stop at Kmart to buy underwear. It was a good thing that was a hypomanic day, but it floored me for the rest of that day and the next. And it started a cycle of bipolar up-and-down oscillations that were clearly related to spoon usage.

My spate of social endeavors started with a double-header. On Saturday I had lunch with a friend at a favorite restaurant I almost never get to go to. We talked about politics, social issues, and book proposals. Then I went home and had a little nap.

That evening Dan and I went to Monkey Bones for Zombie Dogz. I know that takes a little explaining. Monkey Bones is the tattoo studio where I got my semicolon tattoo. Zombie Dogz is a local food truck. Also, it's fun to say "We went to Monkey Bones for Zombie Dogz."

Notice that in a single day I had to get up, out of bed, and get dressed twice. That's a lot of spoons. Sunday I was not able to get out of bed at all.

Monday did not involve socializing, but it was another hellacious spoon-eater. Dan and I spent the day scrounging for documents and information that the IRS wanted. It was taxing. (See what I did there?)

Tuesday was an extra-special social event, though it did not involve getting dressed and going out, or even interacting with other people. It was Jenny Lawson's online book launch party. Better known as the Bloggess, Jenny has severe social anxiety. At this stage in my life, I certainly would not be able to dress up, mingle, and make polite conversation with both friends and complete strangers. The online party was a genius idea.

I sat at home in my pajamas with some red wine while the Bloggess read chapters from her new book, *Furiously Happy*. You should get it, by the way. It's about mental illness, but funny. As low-key a social situation as that was, it still used up spoons because it was something I had never done before. Making sure I had the right URL, converting Central Time to Eastern, not being able to ask questions because I didn't Tweet, worrying that Dan was getting bored. Not a lot a lot of spoons, but still some.

The effects were getting cumulative. Again, I was unable to get out of bed the next day. In fact, Dan and I both slept away most of the daylight hours. For him it's understandable because he works third shift, but I have no such excuse. Except that if you borrow from the next day's spoons, or try to keep going without them, you will pay.

Thursday, I was determined, with or without spoons, I was going to meet a friend for coffee. I've seen her only once, briefly, in several years. In a way, it was a test of my ability to maintain anything approaching a real social life.

I put forth the extra effort because a mutual friend cut her ties with me because I canceled so often on social engagements. I suppose I really have nothing to prove to anyone but myself, but it seems important that I do so. It's not like coffee with a friend is an ordeal or anything. It's just that I know I'll be using a spoon for more than stirring my coffee.

And I hope I have enough spoons left over to work on my *other* blog. (janetcobur.wordpress.com)

I May Have Miscounted My Spoons

THIS WEEK I actually got out of the house, going for lunch and a little shopping with an old friend. Another friend of mine calls these "pants days" because they obviously require putting on pants, for going out farther than the mailbox.

After less than three hours I went home, did some work, and promptly collapsed. All told, I think I was either active, sociable, or some combination thereof for at most four or five hours. That for me is an exceptional day of fortitude, stamina, spoons, and hypomania.

However, I have gotten myself into a situation that will require much more than that. I am going to a writer's conference. Three days of thrill-packed seminars, lunches and dinners, and other business and social-type events. I've done half-day business meetings lately, but nothing so extended, crowded, or spoon-depleting. It will hit a lot of my anxiety triggers: crowds, noise, small talk, social events, and more. I know that by the time we gather for dinner in the evening, I'll already be extra crispy.

The three days of the conference will not allow for much of any downtime, although I have fantasized about asking someone who's staying in the hotel if I can borrow a room for an afternoon nap. The conference is local, so I don't have a room of my own or it wouldn't be a problem. Less of one, anyway. All I'd have to do would be pick which seminars to skip. But the idea of asking a relative stranger for the use of a room or the idea of a relative stranger letting me use a room is pretty ludicrous. Fortunately, I have to get the car home by 10:00 p.m. so my husband can go to work. That means I can't stay for the after-hours socializing, even though that's said to be one of the highlights. But it does mean I get a few more hours in pjs instead of pants.

Back before I had my most recent major meltdown, I was able to attend business conventions and do at least most of the requisite functions. I could and did give little talks at power breakfasts or afternoon cocktail parties, even opened with a joke. I could meet and greet the public at our booth, "howdy and shake," as my father would have called it. I could have lunch with potential writers. I could almost interact with our sales force.

Those days are long past. So now I ask myself, how can I build up my stamina for the writer's conference? Maybe it's time for me to try to reclaim some of those parts of myself.

It feels like I'm going to be training for a marathon, or maybe the Normandy invasion. I know that in order to get through it, I will have to prepare in advance: writing my Sunday blog posts before the conference starts, assembling my wardrobe, checking out the parking situation, stocking up on business cards, and all the other little details that make me so frantic at the last minute.

Perhaps during the next two months I can keep track of how many pants days I'm able to have and gradually increase them. Perhaps I can try to work up to three pants days in a row. Perhaps I can arrange more lunches and shoppings. Perhaps I can improve my usual record of doing only one major thing per day.

The conference itself is certainly a massive and major incentive. Plus, I've already paid for it. Yet another reason to get myself in shape to take advantage of it.

Right now, the conference looks like rather an ordeal, but I hope that by the time it rolls around I'll be in good enough shape to both enjoy it and benefit from it. At least it'll be a group of writers, and humor writers at that. They're known for being at least a little odd. Maybe I'll fit right in. I'll be the one napping on a couch in the hotel lobby in fuzzy slippers. And pants.

A Crowd-Hater at a Conference

"**I'M GONNA KICK BUTT** at this writers' conference!"

I was a *wee* bit manicky.

"I am a writer and I know it! I've had articles published in lots of magazines! I have two blogs and I write in them every week! I can do this!"

It was a conference for humor writers.

"I *know* I can do this! I've written funny things about ratatouille and possums and being burgled by Frenchmen."

So, comes the conference... at a time when I'm not the least bit manicky.

Forget what I said about having developed a few social skills. I was there alone, and confronted with a large group, not small groups or individuals.

And I had paid a lot of money to attend.

It was noisy. It was people-y. It had multiple panels scheduled all day. Every day lunch was an Event with big round tables. Every dinner was an Event with big round tables and important speakers. Everyone there blogged daily or had three blogs, an agent, and/or a book contract.

What to do?

Give myself permission to do what I could do. And skip the other stuff. Ignore the money. Build in breaks. Find quiet spaces. Admit when I'm exhausted and go home.

This is how I got through it all. Or most of it, anyway.

Do what I could. I combed the program book for Sessions I Must Attend, Sessions I Would Like to Attend, and Sessions I Can Skip. Then I looked for sessions that were offered more than once and decided which offering fit my schedule better. I tried to avoid more than two back-to-back sessions.

Ignore the money. Yeah, I paid quite a chunk of change for this, but it would have been ridiculous for me to calculate how much money each session was worth and try to make back my investment. I had to tell myself that I spent a lump sum and that whatever I got from the conference was worth it.

Build in breaks. The conference had what they called breaks – 15 minutes between sessions when everyone rushed the snack tables, compared schedules, and chattered up a storm. My idea of a break was to sit in the lobby in a comfy chair, stare at the program book so no one interrupted me, and carry snacks with me (boxes of raisins are good).

Find quiet spaces. When I needed something quieter than a hotel or conference center lobby, I searched for unused classrooms. In a hotel, the bar is usually pretty empty during a conference and is a good place to sit and relax with a nice glass of iced tea and maybe even complementary peanuts. Sometimes I was lucky enough to find that if I went to the room I wanted for the next session, it would be empty or contain only a few people. When all else fails, there are always the restroom stalls. Unless there's a line.

Leave when exhausted. On the last full day of the conference I found myself slumped in a chair in the lobby, totally wrung out. There were events scheduled that evening that sounded fun and that I had signed up for while manicky. But I just couldn't. The events were mostly entertainment rather than educational anyway, and I was not in a headspace where I could absorb entertainment. The fact that there was a flu going around made my disappearance more understandable, even though I wasn't physically sick.

So, did I learn anything at the conference? Did I make new friends? Did I come back revitalized?

Sort of. I learned that the one-on-one "speed dating" with experts was perhaps the most valuable thing I did. I learned that showing up early for a session allowed me the opportunity to meet one of my idols, the speaker, and spend a little time with her and a small group before the session started. I learned that if I sat near the door it was easier to slip out when panic struck.

I even learned a thing or two about writing: how to write a better query letter, how to improve my blogs, when to consider self-publishing, and so forth. I learned that, despite my manicky expectations, I was no better or worse than the other attendees. We all had skills and valuable experiences and we all had things to learn.

Did I make a lot of new writing friends? No. At least not then. The conference had a Facebook page for attendees and I got involved afterward, online, where I am more comfortable than in crowds. I recognized names I had seen on nametags and had conversations with them. I posted some material from my blogs and read what others posted. I commented and read comments. I "followed" some of the instructors. I read books that attendees had recommended.

To tell the truth, I think I got more from the conference after it was over than when it was going on.

Am I glad I went? Yes. The experience was good for me in more ways than one. Paying attention to my own limits and not trying to live up to artificial expectations made for a good, and survivable, learning experience.

The Therapeutic Hug

THE COMMON WISDOM is that a person needs four hugs a day for survival, eight for maintenance, and 12 for growth. I doubt that this is confirmed by any scientific studies and I doubt that it is true. If it were, there would be millions of people on Earth who would not survive.

I would be one of them. Despite being married to one of the two truly world-class huggers I've met in my life, I do not get my four-a-day. And certainly not 12. Assuming eight hours a day for sleep and eight hours a day for work that would leave eight hours to work in twelve hugs. That's one and a half hugs per hour, and I suspect half a hug just won't do.

In fact, I know it won't. Scientific research *has* been done on the 20-second hug. It releases oxytocin, a pleasure and bonding chemical in the brain. Half a hug would need to be 40 seconds long to do the proper amount of good, and young lovers and newlyweds tend to be the only people who give hugs of that duration.

Then there's the question of what constitutes a hug. For greatest oxytocin effect, I would recommend the full body hug, toe to toe, torso to torso, heads on shoulders, arms tightly squeezing. But you probably can't give that particular hug when you run into an acquaintance in the supermarket, especially not 20 seconds worth, without blocking the aisles.

Other variations of hugs that may be less effective are the side-by-side one-shoulder squeeze (and the multi-person variant, the Big Group Hug), the manly back-thumping, and the A-frame hug (standing a distance apart and leaning in for a hug from the shoulders up). Then there are the virtual hug, usually written ((hug)), with the number of parens indicating the length/intensity of the hug, and the proxy hug, in which you delegate a person to pass along a hug when you're not able to be there. None of these seem really conducive to the 20-second, made-for-thriving hug.

But, on some level, we know that hugs are therapeutic. Oxytocin or whatever, they make us feel better. Lots of hugging goes on at support and 12-step groups, and people who go to those daily might indeed make their recommended quota.

I go to private psychotherapy, however. I've never hugged my therapist and am not even sure whether it's appropriate for therapist and client to hug. It would be awkward to ask, "Can I have a hug?" only to hear, "No. That's unethical." But I suppose it depends on the therapist and the client and how each feels about the subject. I know sex between a therapist and client is unethical, but hugs may be a gray area. Perhaps someone can enlighten me.

Of course, there are people who do not like to, or are afraid to, touch other people. Think Sheldon Cooper on *The Big Bang Theory*. People who are aware of and skilled in responding to others' body language may be able to see the little, or, let's face it, large, cringe when one person sees another moving forward with open arms. If the non-hugger is quick enough, he or she can quickly stick out a hand for a hearty handshake, or the potential hugger will abort the hug and retreat to a friendly tap on the shoulder.

But there are people who will swoop in and envelop you in an unwanted embrace and maybe even air kisses with smacking noises. I suspect these would be more likely to shut down oxytocin entirely, and possibly release adrenaline instead in a fight-or-flight response.

As with sex, the safest route is to ask for consent ("Can I have a hug?") and take no ("I'd rather not") for an answer, without taking offense or pressuring ("Aw, c'mon") and making things even more awkward.

Still, the best advice I can give is to be proactive about hugging. Say, "I need a hug" when you do. Ask "Do you need/want a hug?" when a person you know seems to be in distress.

Avoid hugging strangers, though. That hardly ever helps. At least wait until you've been properly introduced.

Chapter 9: Issues – My Take

A Tattoo Is for Life… • Those Who Will Not See • The Answer to Bullying • Owning My Bullying • Yes, I Am Crazy. Thanks for Asking. • Read Your Way to Sanity • Diagnosis and Dickinson • Is My Cat Bipolar? • Response to the Dalai Lama • My Second Mental Health Tattoo * I Chose Fat Over Misery • Who's a Spoonie?

A Tattoo Is for Life...

...**THIS ONE,** especially so.

As soon as I learned about the semicolon tattoo, I knew I had to get one, and not just because I'm a huge grammar nerd. Because I'm bipolar and want to spread the word about mental health issues.

In writing, the semicolon indicates a place where a writer could have finished a sentence, but instead chose to go on. This makes the semicolon an effective and beautiful symbol for suicide prevention efforts and those who struggle with mental disorders.

Every day we choose to get out of bed; choose to take our medications; choose to make and go to our therapist appointments; choose to live another day; and choose to go on with our story.

This is not something I invented. Here are the people behind it: http://www.projectsemicolon.com/. And here are some stories about the phenomenon that have been working their way through the media and around the internet.

Here is my story.

I am possibly the last person you would ever expect to get a tattoo. I am probably the last person *I* would ever expect to get a tattoo. I'm in my 50s, a former English teacher, married for over 30 years, fond of reading and word puzzles and cats.

Nevertheless, the professionals at Monkey Bones Tattoos in Beavercreek, OH, did not seem surprised when I showed up one day and presented my wrist. When I explained what I wanted – to put down a deposit and book an appointment to get a semicolon tattoo – I learned that they had a cancellation and could ink me right away.

What the hell, I thought. *Might as well*. I had learned about the tattoos about a month before and had thought it over plenty. It was by no means a spur-of-the-moment (or drunken) impulse.

Mike Guidone showed me into his studio and explained the procedure.

He presented me with stencils of three different sizes of semicolons. I chose the in-between one. My wrist is fairly small, so the big one would have looked out of place, but the small one wasn't noticeable enough. The idea is for people to see it and ask, so you can share the meaning and talk to them about mental health and combatting the stigma.

I sat in the dentist-type chair, listened to a brief explanation, got answers to some questions, and was ready to start.

Did it hurt? Not particularly. It was a feeling between a scratch and a sting and took only about ten minutes. Some aftercare instructions and I was done.

Then I paid ($80, the shop minimum), tipped Mike, and was on my way. Now I care for the tattoo while it heals, anointing it with unscented lotion several times a day, avoiding sunlight or soaking, and trying my very best not to scratch or pick at it.

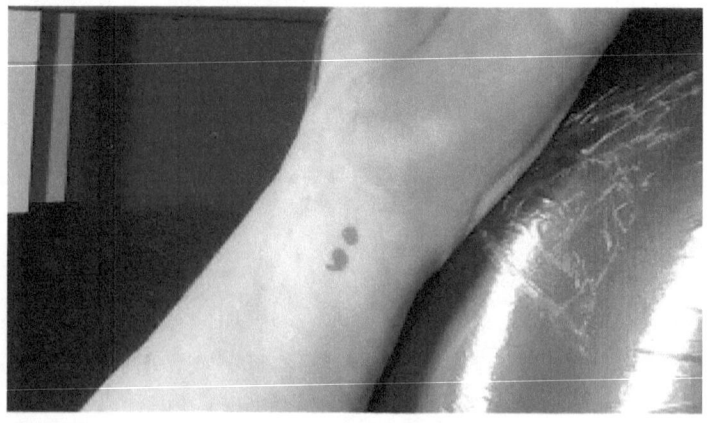

The results.
Am I happy with it? You bet!
And, like I said, it's for life! My story isn't finished yet.

Those Who Will Not See

ONCE I SHARED a post on Facebook that I thought was awesome. Here it is, so you can contemplate it too: http://momastery.com/blog/2014/01/30/share-schools/

The comments I got on it were things like "Wow! Brilliant!" and "This would have changed my life."

A friend posted exactly the same essay, and here are some of the responses he got, interspersed with comments I made.

> **COMMENT:** Wow, a math teacher that does not understand how game theory works. That is kind of sad.
> **COMMENT:** It should be noted that the premiss [sic] of revenge is that 1+1=0.
> **ME:** Why are you debating game theory? This is about the human heart.
> **COMMENT:** If she's optimizing to prevent a low probability event, she's making the same mistake as the TSA.
> **ME:** Summarize in no more than three words what this essay is about. Kids. Loneliness. Ostracism. Help the hurting. Pay attention, gang. The point is zooming by somewhere overhead. The TSA is irrelevant to this.
> **COMMENT:** I think that people who think that by mining a lot of data and then look for correlations they can detect who's being abusive are...naive at best, dangerous at worst.
> **ME:** I'll take naive over uncaring any day. A teacher that cares is way more important than the TSA, NSA, and all those TLA [Three-Letter Acronym] people. I'm leaving now before I say something that will get me

banned. [The poster blocks or bans anyone who engages in ad hominem or other abusive attacks.]
COMMENT: This is a single teacher data mining, yes. The NSA at least has some experience in doing it correctly...

Of course, there were other people who responded to what the post was <u>about</u>, but I was appalled at the number who skipped right past the topic in favor of showing off their erudition instead of compassion.

Admittedly, I'm a professional nitpicker, and I have sometimes been guilty of the same thing, ignoring the content of a post to go after incorrect usage of "literally," for example. But my God, the relentless refusal to address the topic, even when it was pointed out repeatedly, and not just by me, that they were discussing Something Else Entirely. With rants so long they were essays themselves, and links to articles on the NSA and how to avoid being arrested. The thread included comments on profiling as well.

I have been a victim of bullying, etc. So have many of the people who commented when I shared the essay, and when they passed it along. So have many people who tried to get my friend's comment thread back on topic.

And so, too, I suspect, were at least some of the people who nattered on about statistical analysis and all the other extraneous matters. I cannot imagine them going through school without getting taunted, threatened, or beaten up for being a "smarty-pants," "brainiac," or "know-it-all," or some words less polite. And I suspect that those people are in MASSIVE denial, still trying to build themselves a shield of facts and statistics and analysis and theories and showy buzzwords.

I would tell them, if they would listen, which they likely wouldn't, that this strategy won't work. I know. I've tried it. Again and again. And yet again.

What is that definition of mental illness? Oh yes. Doing the same thing over and over and expecting different results.

So, what's the point? The topic, as it were? I may be crazy. But by the above definition, so are they. And I'm getting treatment for it, not reinforcing myself with a feedback loop. Oops. Did I just get pedantic and jargon-y? I'll stop now and apologize.

The Answer to Bullying

"**BEING BULLIED** is not a harmless rite of passage or an inevitable part of growing up; it has serious long-term consequences," says Stephen Luntz in an article, "Study Finds Bullying Affects Mental Health More Than Child Abuse" [http://www.iflscience.com/brain/price-bullying-measured].

Well, duh.

But wait. Look at that title again. "Bullying Affects Mental Health *More Than Child Abuse*"?

Yes. That's an accurate headline, not just clickbait.

"Our results showed those who were bullied were more likely to suffer from mental health problems than those who were maltreated," says Professor Dieter Wolke of the University of Warwick in the article. "Being both bullied and maltreated also increased the risk of overall mental health problems, anxiety and depression."

He adds, "It is important for schools, health services and other agencies to work together to reduce bullying and the adverse effects related to it."

Again, duh. Easier said than done.

And how big is the problem? A CBS News poll reports that most Americans reported being bullied at some point while growing up. Only 41 percent report never being bullied.

"Just" 10 percent said they were bullied "a lot." That's still a lot of children who are bullied a lot.

I know I was. And I'm willing to bet that many of you were, too.

So, what's to be done?

Well, we know what doesn't work.

Telling those who are bullied:

"They're just joking."
"Learn to take a little teasing."
"You're too sensitive." (my personal favorite)
"Learn to fight back."
"Get used to it."
"Just ignore it."
"What they say doesn't matter."
"Don't let them see that they hurt you."
"Laugh it off."
"Handle it yourself."
"Try to make friends with them."
"Give them what they want and they'll leave you alone."
"Don't give them what they want and they'll stop."
"Stay away from them."
"Stand up to them."
"Get your friends together when they're around."
"Tell your parents/teacher/principal."
"Take karate lessons."
"Avoid the second floor bathroom (or wherever)."
"Grow up."

Look again at that list. They are pieces of advice to the VICTIMS of bullying on HOW NOT TO BE BULLIED. What's wrong with this picture?

Feminists and their allies have begun questioning the advice given to women on HOW NOT TO BE RAPED. Instead, they say, the focus should be on teaching men HOW NOT TO BE RAPISTS.

And apparently, this approach is having some success.

Of course, bullying is not rape; the analogy breaks down quickly. But both are about power and "the other," asserting dominance over someone who is different.

In bullying, that difference can be real or merely perceived, and can be literally anything – weight, height, intelligence, socioeconomic level, race, ethnicity, popularity, clothing, sex, gender, hair color, disability, athletic prowess, speech, preference of superhero. The criteria for who is a victim seem completely arbitrary, because they are. The victim is the other, someone who is by definition different.

Is it fair, or even reasonable, to tell victims to alter whatever it is about themselves that makes them different? It can be soul-killing to have to pretend you are not smart, not poor, not gay, not Muslim. It can be impossible to pretend you're not short, don't have a disability, are good at sports. And why should victims have to, any more than women should never go out alone at night or never flirt?

We need to start teaching kids HOW NOT TO BE BULLIES, not how not to be bullied.

Some specifics, like this:
"If you think another kid is gay, ignore it."
"If someone is not as popular as you, so what?"
"If a kid in your class dresses funny, don't say anything."
"If it's not fun for everyone, stop."

Or this:
"Don't hit people because you don't like the way they look."
"Don't joke about people who don't enjoy it."
"Don't call people anything but what they want to be called."
"If someone is unhappy, don't make it worse."

Or this:
"If someone is smarter or less smart than you, form a study group."
"If someone has less money than you, do things that don't cost money."

"If someone is always dropping her books, help pick them up."

I'm not an educator or a child psychologist, just a former smart, scrawny girl with weird hair and poor eyesight. In other words, bully-bait. **Childhood depression and bullying are two of my primary concerns when it comes to mental health and society. Relentlessly bullied as a child, to the point where other students threw rocks at me, I remained on the defensive for a lot of my life. This sort of thing will make you wary of friendship and even more likely to isolate. None of which makes it any easier to join the popular crowd, or any crowd, for that matter.**

Maybe my ideas won't work. But what we're doing now sure doesn't. That poll I mentioned earlier suggests that bullying is actually increasing, despite all the attention the topic is getting. Generalities like "All people deserve your respect" and "Celebrate differences" and "Be-kind-keep-your-hands-to-yourself-no-hazing-no-fighting-no-name-calling" aren't getting the job done.

Bully culture is well and truly entrenched in our society. To change that, we need to change the culture if for no other reason than to head off all those mental health problems waiting up ahead for bullied children.

Who's with me?

Owning My Bullying

I HAVE WRITTEN many times before this on the subject of bullying – and now I have to admit that I have been a bully too.

Bullying is often seen in stereotypical terms as a larger kid extorting money from a smaller, weaker one, or tormenting someone in the locker room with "swirlies" and other indignities. But there are many kinds of bullying. There is physical bullying, the kind most people think of. There is ostracism or social bullying, the stereotype of which is the clique of mean girls or arrogant jocks. There are racist bullying, ethnic bullying, socioeconomic bullying, ableist bullying, sexual bullying, and just about any other type you can name.

Nowadays, one of the most vicious types of bullying, with the most harmful and longest-lasting effects, is cyberbullying. The tools of connection are being used to separate, exclude, and destroy reputations and even lives.

None of those is the kind of bully I was.

I was an intellectual bully. And since I realized that, only recently, I am ashamed.

I am not ashamed of my intelligence or my educational accomplishments. Those were the products of nature and nurture that I had little control over. It was what I did with those advantages that is shameful.

I used my smarts and my vocabulary to squash other students.

It may have started as a defense against the bullying I received, physical, social, and whatever else. Intelligence seemed like the only weapon I had, and I wielded it as one. I was taking revenge in the only way I knew how. And that is something I should never have done.

I may not have intended it that way, but every snarky remark, every intellectual put-down, every sesquipedalian word flung back at my bullies carried a message. I was telling them that they were stupid and inferior, and that I was smarter, better, than they were.

If that's not bullying, I don't know what is. And I'm sure it caused damage to egos and self-esteem, as well as perpetuating the cycle of be-bullied-and-bully that leaves countless perpetrators and victims in its wake.

Later in life, as my bipolar disorder deepened, I turned the bullying inward. I made self-deprecating remarks, snarked at myself, even made fun of myself for being overeducated and pedantic. I thought I had to do these things to myself before someone else did them to me. It was at once a measure of my profoundly low self-esteem and a way to lower it even further.

In essence I was bullying myself. And I've known other people who have done likewise. For what it's worth, I've since learned that it can be profoundly irritating to listen to a person tear himself or herself down this way.

Intellectual bullying is a hard habit to break. The words, the ideas, the sarcasm are there for the using. The consequence, of course, is driving people away, sometimes without even realizing it. I have done this and seen it only when looking back at the potential or actual friends lost, the coworkers who thought I was a jerk, the people I've hurt.

I've been trying to break myself of the habit. Oddly, the Internet helps. It is, as has been noted, true that there are few ways to convey tone of voice in chat or email. There is no sarcasm font. But there are ways to let the recipient know that you do not mean a message literally or unkindly. You can place <snerk> after a remark or a :P emoji or a sticker that demonstrates you mean well. I've even seen people use <sarcasm on> and <sarcasm off> around their messages to make them clearer.

But mostly, I try to guard my speech. I have to install a little censor (or sensor) that says, "Ooh! That's funny! But is it insulting?" before I make a remark.

I'd rather pause for a second and look like a doof than go back to being a bully.

Yes, I Am Crazy. Thanks for Asking.

I CARE A LOT about people's perception of mental illness, but more for other people than myself. Call someone in the news a nutjob, or worse, a psycho, and my insult antenna go up and I launch into a diatribe on the correct usage of psychiatric terms and how they are often misused in a way that perpetuates societal fear and mistrust of mental illnesses and those who have them.

But call me a nutjob? That's something entirely different.

I've been called a lot of things in my time, from schoolyard taunts (loony tunes, weirdo) to psychiatric labels (clinically depressed, bipolar 2). This used to bother me, but anymore, I don't mind.

It's not because of the old saying, "Sticks and stones can break my bones, but words will never hurt me." We all know that's a damn filthy lie. I think it's because I've developed a sense of humor about the "crazy" thing. If Al Yankovic can embrace "Weird," I can embrace "squirrel-bait" or "wacko." Even "bat-shit" or "bug-fuck" crazy don't get me riled, though many find them offensive, and I can't fault them for that. Everyone has a different level of tolerance and sense of what's funny.

Take, for example, the time when my friend gave me a t-shirt that said, "Leave Me Alone. I'm Having a Crisis." Her husband was dubious about the gift, thinking that I would be offended. I wasn't. My friend thought it was a hoot and so did I. I just bought a t-shirt that says, "You Won't Believe the Crazy Shit That Happens Next..." I'm going to wear it to my next psychotherapist appointment. I also have one that says, "What If the Light at the End of the Tunnel Is an Oncoming Freight Train?"

I admit to being disconcerted when publicly confronted by a person who asks, "Are you the one there's something wrong with?" or "Do you have mental problems?" In the first case, the elderly gentleman was thinking of my sister-in-law, who had MS, and in the second, the person recognized me from the psychiatrist's waiting room. But I'm not offended. Mostly I regret that I didn't have snappy come-backs. I thought of some great ones later.

There are still some assumptions that do offend or at least irritate me. I'm not going to walk into a fast food outlet and start shooting up the place. Mania is not fun. I've decided not to reproduce, but nobody can tell me that I shouldn't.

Oh, and there's one other thing. In the past, when I've mentioned my mood disorder to acquaintances or co-workers, they feel obliged to take my emotional temperature five times a day. "Are you okay? How are you feeling?" So, I would add to the list: Not all people with bipolar disorder are rapid cycling.

So, am I crazy? Yes. But I don't think that's necessarily a bad thing. Most people use the word "crazy" to describe how they feel when they're in love. And I'm good with that.

My Second Mental Health Tattoo

ONCE AGAIN, I have gotten a tattoo, supporting the cause of mental health.

A few months ago, I became a part of what's called the semicolon project. For those of you who aren't up on the terminology, a semicolon tattoo represents mental health awareness, especially erasing the stigma, and suicide prevention.

My new tattoo represents bipolar disorder. Again, it's made up of punctuation: two colons and a paren. These symbols, unlike the semicolon, have no special meaning in writing and are never seen together in that order. Instead they make up a double emoticon: Looked at one way, the colon and paren make up a smiley face. Looked at the other way, a frowny face.

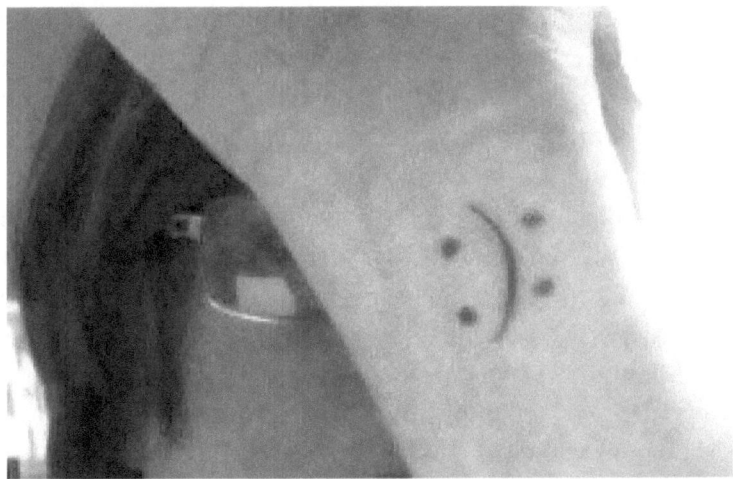

This symbolism is easier for anyone seeing the tattoo to grasp. In a way, it's a minimalist version of the comedy and tragedy masks you often see in theaters.

Again, it's a conversation starter. Bipolar disorder is not well understood by the general public. This is particularly true of bipolar disorder type 2, the kind I have, which many people have never even heard of.

Since I have gone public with having a mental illness, it seems only appropriate to introduce people to the disorder in a way that's creative, nonthreatening, and understandable. It's a lot less abrupt than blurting out, "Hey, I have a mental illness!" Even my mother-in-law recognizes that these tattoos are not just a whim, but for a good cause.

The second tattoo is on my right wrist, so no matter which hand I extend, I can open up new understanding about a very real problem that many people live with daily.

A number of articles have come out lately questioning whether a person who gets a tattoo will regret it when they grow older. I think I can say with complete confidence that I will never regret these tattoos. They say something about who I am, something that will not change as I grow older. The disorder will always be with me and so will these symbols. For the rest of my life I can use them to educate, identify with other bipolar people, and remind myself that wrists are not for cutting.

I will say, however, that whoever thinks of these things had better put the brakes on new mental health-related tattoo designs, especially those made of punctuation, or I will soon become the Illustrated Editor/Blogger. At the moment I have no plans for any further ink. My friends, however, tell me that tattoos are addictive. So, we'll see.

A few notes, since everyone asks: These simple tattoos take 10 minutes or less to apply. They hurt a little bit, but not much. A stinging sensation. They may fade a bit at first and need a touch-up. Because they are so quick and simple, you will not pay a lot to have them done. After you get the tattoo you have to take care of it while it heals, moisturizing it regularly for the first 3-6 weeks or so.

If you decide to get a tattoo, check out the studio before you have it done. It should be a professional operation, with high standards of cleanliness and concern for health. Tattoo artists should wear surgical gloves and change them frequently. There may be a consent form to fill out, indicating that you know what you are getting into, and even indicating whether you have various medical conditions or allergies, or have drunk alcohol within the previous eight hours. A reputable tattoo studio will not work on a drunken client.

Do you have a tattoo related to mental health? I'd love to hear about it. But don't tell me if it's more punctuation. I only have two wrists.

Read Your Way to Sanity

AS REPORTED IN *Smithsonian* magazine, "Doctors are now prescribing books to patients with depression, hoping that reading will help them find connections."

First, let's note that this is third-hand information, from the U.K. National Health Service to the *Boston Globe* to the *Smithsonian*. Fourth-hand, if you count this book. Many of the details and even the explanation of the concept may have lost quite a bit in the transitions. But here are the basics:

If your primary care physician diagnoses you with "mild to moderate" depression, one of her options is now to scribble a title on a prescription pad. You take the torn-off sheet not to the pharmacy but to your local library, where it can be exchanged for a copy of "Overcoming Depression," "Mind Over Mood," or "The Feeling Good Handbook."

There are also books prescribed for other conditions including, I presume, bipolar disorder. And they sound a lot the old self-help books of the sorts we read in the 1970s, of the *Women Who Are Ambivalent About Women Against Women Against Feminism* sort (h/t The Bloggess for that awesome title).

Back then I was diagnosed with depression, and back then the Common Wisdom said, "Depression is anger turned inward." Now that we know more about brain biochemistry, neurotransmitters, and such, advice from a book called "Mind Over Mood" is not likely to be all that much help. And God spare me from anything called "The Feeling Good Handbook."

Of course, the Brits' prescriptions are not actual bibliotherapy, which is a real thing, defined by The American Library Association thusly:

> The use of books selected on the basis of content in a planned reading program designed to facilitate the recovery of patients suffering from mental illness or emotional disturbance. Ideally, the process occurs in three phases: personal identification of the reader with a particular character in the recommended work, resulting in psychological catharsis, which leads to rational insight concerning the relevance of the solution suggested in the text to the reader's own experience. Assistance of a trained psychotherapist is advised.

This is a much better idea, but again, it's advisable to check the publication dates on those books. The extremely popular book *I Never Promised You a Rose Garden* was written before anyone really knew about the genetic and biological components of schizophrenia.

I'm sure there is modern fiction that would be useful in bibliotherapy. Personally, I think that the Dementors in J.K. Rowling's Harry Potter books provide as good a description of depression as I've ever heard:

> [T]hey glory in decay and despair, they drain peace, hope, and happiness out of the air around them... Get too near a Dementor and every good feeling, every happy memory will be sucked out of you. ... You will be left with nothing but the worst experiences of your life.

Rowling herself has spoken about the connection:

> It was entirely conscious. And entirely from my own experience. Depression is the most unpleasant thing I have ever experienced. It is that absence of being able

to envisage that you will ever be cheerful again. The absence of hope. That very deadened feeling, which is so very different from feeling sad. Sad hurts but it's a healthy feeling. It's a necessary thing to feel. Depression is very different. I think [dementors] are the scariest things I've written.

As for me, I find insight into mental disorders primarily in nonfiction, though not necessarily in books with a psychiatric or psychological perspective. *The Noonday Demon: An Atlas of Depression* by Andrew Solomon is, I think, essential for any collection. It combines the author's own experiences with historical, cultural, philosophical, and other ways people have thought and written about depression.

Generally, though, I prefer memoirs of people who have lived through or with the conditions they write about. Although my diagnosis is bipolar disorder type 2, I also read memoirs about people with other conditions. There are many similarities of experiences, symptoms, feelings, and other aspects that I find familiar or helpful.

Being an ardent bibliophile as well as a psychiatric patient, I believe in the potential of bibliotherapy. Being a former consumer of self-help books, I sincerely doubt *that* genre will do much good.

Diagnosis and Dickinson

The Brain — is wider than the Sky —
For — put them side by side —
The one the other will contain
With ease — and You — beside —
The Brain is deeper than the sea —
For — hold them — Blue to Blue —
The one the other will absorb —
As Sponges — Buckets — do —
The Brain is just the weight of God —
For — Heft them — Pound for Pound —
And they will differ — if they do —
As Syllable from Sound

— Emily Dickinson

I RAN ACROSS this poem in a book called *Shrinks: The Untold Story of Psychiatry* and it made me think.

Dickinson was, by all accounts, a recluse. She seldom went out and, when visitors came, she sometimes sat behind a screen while she talked to them. She never dared to submit her poems for publication. Fewer than a dozen were published in her lifetime, and those only because someone else submitted them without her knowledge. Her wealthy, loving family sheltered and nurtured her so that she never had to face the outside world.

Emily Dickinson had Social Anxiety Disorder.

And Abraham Lincoln suffered clinical depression. So did Charles Dickens.

Bipolar sufferers include Beethoven, Schumann, and Isaac Newton.

Charles Darwin, Michelangelo, and Nikola Tesla were all obsessive-compulsive.

Autism, dyslexia, and various learning disabilities affected Einstein, Galileo, Mozart, and even General Patton.

And Van Gogh! Let me tell you about Van Gogh. He had epilepsy. Or depression. Or psychotic attacks. Or bipolar disorder. Or possibly some combination thereof.

I call bullshit. I'm not saying none of those people had assorted mental disorders. My point is that we can't tell from this distance in time.

In none of these cases, as far as I know, did any of the aforementioned people see a psychiatrist, psychoanalyst, psychotherapist, or even a phrenologist. None were diagnosed with any psychiatric condition, and no record of such a diagnosis has come down to us from any reliable source. Some even lived before psychiatry was invented.

People – mental health workers, but also art and literary critics, biographers, and the general public – have looked at these extraordinary people's lives and work and decided that their behavior and their art *look like* those of a person who *might be* bipolar or obsessive-compulsive or psychotic. They also like to retro-diagnose physical conditions there is no record of or only vague names for. King Tut, Henry VIII, and Napoleon are particularly good theoretical patients.

Why the tendency to ascribe mental disorders to famous people? I can see two reasons, beyond the thrill of solving a mystery and feeling clever.

The first is the old saying about there being a thin line between madness and genius. These historical figures were geniuses, so they must have been mad. Or as we say now, suffering from mental disorders.

The other is the need for role models and inspiration. If Van Gogh could become one of the most famous artists ever (though not successful in his own lifetime), you too may rise above, even use, your disorder to accomplish greatness.

It's possible, I guess, but it's not likely. Certainly, those with mental disorders can aspire to *and achieve* rich, full lives, satisfying relationships and jobs and artistic pursuits. These are the ordinary accomplishments of ordinary people, both with and without mental illness, and it's a small miracle that people can achieve any one or more of these. Not everyone does, again, with or without mental troubles or psychiatric diagnoses.

And for me, at least, it's enough.

Can the spark of imaginative genius strike a person with a mental disorder? Of course. Can that person succeed and achieve lasting fame? Maybe, though the odds aren't good. Is a person saying, "Look, I can be Van Gogh!" likely to fall short? Almost certainly. Can that failure to achieve greatness make a person feel worse about himself or herself instead of better? You tell me.

There's nothing wrong with aiming high, and there's nothing that says a person with a psychiatric diagnosis can't do just that. It's a good idea for anyone. As one of Lois McMaster Bujold's characters says, "Aim high. You may still miss the target but at least you won't shoot your foot off."

But pinning your hopes on a similarity with a non-psychiatric, perhaps non-existent, diagnosis of a genius may not be the best way to get there.

Better to look in these geniuses' work for insights that can help you understand your own condition or pull you through tough times. Here's another of Emily Dickinson's poems that has always spoken to me about the experience of a depressive crisis and its aftermath.

After great pain, a formal feeling comes —
The Nerves sit ceremonious, like Tombs —

The stiff Heart questions 'was it He, that bore,'
And 'Yesterday, or Centuries before'?
The Feet, mechanical, go round —
A Wooden way
Of Ground, or Air, or Ought —
Regardless grown,
A Quartz contentment, like a stone —
This is the Hour of Lead —
Remembered, if outlived,
As Freezing persons, recollect the Snow —
First — Chill — then Stupor — then the letting go —

Was Emily herself depressed? We'll never really know. And as long as we have her poems, I don't really care.

Is My Cat Bipolar?

IT SURE SEEMS like it. She lies around all day, barely moving. Then at any given time she races through the house pursuing nothing at all. Afterward she lies back down, immobilized again. It looks an awful lot like rapid cycling.

I'm not going to get into the debate here of whether animals have emotions or humans are simply anthropomorphizing. Of course, animals have emotions, and act on them. Our cat Maggie could snub you, so you really knew you'd been snubbed. Another cat, Shaker, was mortally offended if you stuck a whisker on the top of her head and made "beep beep" noises. Our dog Bridget had deep anxiety around strangers, both human and canine. She was known to wet herself, or my husband's shoe. Polar bears can experience boredom. I have it on good authority that sheep can hold a grudge.

But can animals experience mental illness? Recently the BBC examined the question in an article by Shreya Dasgupta.

The article is long and rather technical, citing genetic studies I'm not capable of summarizing and using words like "telomere." But the Beeb's resounding answer to the question is yes. Not only can animals feel emotion, they can suffer from mental disorders. The report says:

> To our eyes, many animals seem to suffer from forms of mental illness. Whether they are pets, or animals kept in ill-managed zoos and circuses, they can become excessively sad, anxious, or even traumatised....There is growing evidence that many animals can suffer from mental health disorders similar to those seen in humans.

It was decades ago that I first heard about polar bears on Prozac, due to their pacing obsessively or swimming repetitively back and forth. I did wonder how the vets calculated the dosage: by body weight or brain size or trial and error. Of course, rather than psychotropics, what the bears really needed was more appropriate-sized enclosures.

Stress and social deprivation seem to be two of the factors that can bring on mental illness, particularly depression or PTSD, in animals. Dogs that serve in combat zones have been known to have trouble adjusting to civilian life. And the death of an animal's relative or beloved human companion has been anecdotally linked to profound grief and even death.

The BBC notes that all the evidence we have for animal mental illness comes from pets, captive animals, and research specimens:

> That probably reflects our own preferences for certain animals. "It's the animals that we find very charismatic, like elephants or chimpanzees, or animals that we share our homes with, like dogs," that command our attention, says animal behaviour expert Marc Bekoff.

But do wild animals really suffer from mental disorders? It's practically impossible to tell.

For one thing, wild animals cannot bare their souls to therapists. For many reclusive wild animals, we know so little of what is normal behavior that we would be hard pressed to identify abnormal responses to environmental stressors.

Still, the experts say, even invertebrates like octopi and honeybees seem to suffer from, if not what we would call mental illness, at least maladaptive reactions to trauma.

Severe psychiatric illnesses like schizophrenia seem to go with higher intelligence. Octopi are actually quite smart. But again, how can you tell whether a dolphin is hallucinating? It may be that animals with extreme mental illness are weeded out by evolution, as their erratic behavior may lead to early death and loss of the ability to pass on their genes.

Is this true for humans as well? Are mental illness and intelligence correlated? As yet there is little consensus. Sometimes the debate boils down to chicken-and-egg levels. Do people with lower intelligence experience more depression because they are unable to accomplish what they want to do? Or does depression make it more unlikely that they will accomplish what they wish for? Most of the studies seem to relate to depression.

As the BBC report says, "Mental disorders seem to be the price animals pay for their intelligence. The same genes that made us smart also predisposed us to madness. There's nothing shameful in that."

Except, of course, that in humans there is stigma. Cats, now – they can get away with acting as crazy as they want. We'll just call it adorbz and post it on YouTube.

Response to the Dalai Lama

THIS FRIDAY, my Facebook newsfeed included a quotation from the Dalai Lama.

> Depression seems to be related to fear, anger and frustration. When you're in a bad mood, even if you meet with your friends, you don't take pleasure in their company. But when you're in a good mood, even if things go wrong, you can cope with them without difficulty. This is why putting yourself in a good mood, making a point of developing a sense of loving kindness gives you greater inner strength.

While I respect and admire the Dalai Lama, on this subject he is wrong.

I wrote a blog post to tell him and his followers so. I posted it on Blogher.com. (Blogher is a site for women bloggers that sometimes syndicates content. It is more general than what I usually post in my Bipolar Me blog, so I wrote something special for them.)

As I researched, trying to find when and where the Dalai Lama said this (I couldn't), I discovered several articles about research into depression and Buddhist principles and techniques.

One was an article by Kathy Gilsinan at *The Atlantic*. It talked about "high-amplitude gamma-oscillations in the brain, which are indicative of plasticity." What that is or has to do with depression, I don't know. It sounds like "handwavium" to me.

One that made more sense was this, from Jeanie Lerche Davis at WebMD: (The feature was reviewed by Louise Chang, MD.)

While meditation can help many who are depressed, it's not a sure-fire cure, [Charles W.] Raison [psychiatry professor and co-director of Emory's Collaborative for Contemplative Studies] tells WebMD. "In fact, many people with mood disorders find they can't do meditation when they're depressed." Their thoughts are too overwhelming. They are anxious, nervous, and can't sit – and likely they need antidepressants, he says.

That's more like it.
In my response to the Dalai Lama, I said,

Real, clinical depression is not about being in a "bad mood." It's true that a truly depressed person does not find pleasure even in ordinarily pleasurable things, such as meeting with friends. But we cannot simply put ourselves in a good mood.

That's the hell of depression. We want to enjoy the good times. We want to put ourselves into a place of inner strength. But we can't. Not without help.

In fact, your advice is hurtful to depressed people. Too many times we have been told, "Cheer up." "Smile! You'll feel better." "Think about someone else for a change." "What do you have to feel bad about?"

Don't you think we would if we could?

Remarks like these remind us that we have an illness and we cannot cure ourselves by willpower alone, no more than a person with hepatitis or tuberculosis or even schizophrenia can. We need help, and most of us need medication.

You do a disservice to people with depression when you tell them to put themselves in a good mood. You, an enlightened spiritual leader, may be able to do it, but we can't.

Certainly, we can benefit from practicing loving kindness and developing inner strength.

But without treatment for depression, how many of us can do that?

It angers me when people say that depression – or any mental disorder – is something people can or should be able to cure with an attitude adjustment. I've heard it too many times from people in my life, and I'm sure you have too.

What's really disappointing is that someone like the Dalai Lama, with his legion of followers and enormous credibility, is perpetuating this old way of thinking.

This lie.

I Chose Fat Over Misery

I WAS A SKINNY kid who grew a lot less skinny.

Do my bipolar meds have something to do with that?

Probably.

Do I care?

No.

I've noticed a lot of people with bipolar disorder panicking over the topic of weight gain. "I know I need meds, but I'm afraid of weight gain." "What meds can I take that don't cause weight gain?" "I tried X med, but I quit because of the weight gain."

It's true that mental health and physical health are linked – what affects one may affect the other. And it's true that medications have side effects, among which may be weight gain.

What I don't get is why some people are so afraid of weight gain that they would sacrifice their mental health to avoid it.

Actually I do sort of get it. There are ads everywhere that promote thinness, even to the point of illness, as the ideal for both feminine and masculine. There is a "War on Obesity" and plenty of people who will tell you that your body mass index is the most important number that identifies you. There are fat people jokes and gags that could not be told about any other group, be it race, sex, ethnicity, or religion. Plenty of comedians have made a good living making fun of fat, even their own. On TV, the fat character is never the hero.

Now back to the skinny, scrawny, bony kid I was. Undiagnosed and untreated. Aware that there was something wrong with me, but no idea what.

I had mini-meltdowns and major meltdowns. I had anxious twitches. I burst into tears when certain songs came on the radio, and not necessarily sad ones. "Take Me Home, Country Roads" tore me up. "I Am a Rock" could leave me sobbing. I took walks in the rain till I was soaked to the skin. I would laugh out loud for no reason that anyone else could see.

I was a mess. But a thin one.

It's relatively recently that doctors and scientists have explored the connection between psychotropic medications and weight gain. Some have speculated that people who are depressed don't eat much. Then, when their meds kick in and they feel better, their appetites return. In my case, I ate more when depressed and less when anxious. By the end of my undergraduate years, I was drinking banana milkshakes so my parents wouldn't worry about how thin I was when they saw me at graduation.

Slowly, I got better with therapy and meds. Slowly, I gained weight. At first, I didn't notice. Then I did. I tried prescription diet pills and Lean Cuisine, which worked for a while. But eventually, as is true of most dieters, I started piling the pounds back on. If one of my psychotropics was to blame, I couldn't pinpoint which one, what with going on and off so many different ones and the cocktail of several I ended up with.

But as I got better and gained weight, I also started making friends, going on dates, finding lovers, and eventually meeting the man I would marry. Some of them were overweight, too. But that wasn't what mattered most to them – or to me. Oh, I suppose there were people who were turned off by my well-padded physique. Maybe some of them were marvelous people, and maybe I would have enjoyed their company if they could have seen past the weight.

But the fact is, I now have plenty of close friends who just don't give a damn about weight. Sometimes one of us will need to lose weight for a specific health reason like diabetes, and the rest of us will offer encouragement. But for the most part, we are who we are and love each other that way.

Given the choice, and I do have the choice, I will take the psychotropics that keep me reasonably stable and happy and productive. And yes, overweight. I remember the misery, the despair and pain, and no matter how I look, I don't ever want to go back there. Self-esteem, for me at least, is better if it comes from the inside out, not the other way around.

The bottom line?

I've been skinny. I've been fat. Either way, I'm still me.

Who's a Spoonie?

WITH ALL THE TALK about cultural appropriation lately, I'm hesitant to wear Kokopelli earrings or eat at the Chinese buffet. I understand that some people feel that Canadians playing Englishmen who are pretending to be Japanese for a production of *The Mikado* is offensive or racist. I don't always agree, but I understand the principle involved. Even I, a WASP, find Mickey Rooney's character in *Breakfast at Tiffany's* to be egregious, appalling, and insulting to everyone involved, including the audience.

But recently there's come the claim that those who are not entitled to it are appropriating Spoon Theory language. And in this case, "entitled to it" means someone with an "invisible illness" - chronic pain, chronic fatigue, and other conditions that do not announce themselves to the public with visible cues such as wheelchairs, crutches, missing limbs, or guide dogs.

If you don't already know Spoon Theory, you should. Basically, "spoonies" have only a limited amount of energy units per day, represented by spoons. Spoonies must use a ridiculous number of spoons to get through tasks that others accomplish normally in the course of life - showering, driving to work, driving home, fixing dinner, et endless cetera.

In fact, on any given day a Spoonie may not have enough spoons to get out of bed and get showered and dressed. It's not that Spoonies are lazy; they may have only three metaphoric spoons that day, compared to a non-Spoonie's typical, oh, I don't know, 20? 30?

I have written about whether bipolar disorder and other mental disorders are invisible illnesses. As far as I'm concerned, we're Spoonies and "entitled" to Spoonie language. Most of us have had the experience of not having enough spoons to spend on a morning shower, having to choose between hygiene and, say, eating breakfast.

So now, apparently, the general public is picking up Spoonie language, saying "I'm out of spoons" when they simply mean "I'm tired" or "That was an exhausting day. I'm done." And some Spoonies resent that.

I have two things to say about it. The first is that language is always growing and changing. But it does that on its own, without our control. Unless we're France. France at least tries. We may wish to eradicate the "n-word," but we can't. It's less socially acceptable to use in polite company, but you know people still use it. Read the comments section on any social media post about President Obama if you don't believe me.

The second thing is that Spoon Theory and language are entering the mainstream. People without invisible illnesses are at least getting a clue of what it means. They may not have the details right, but at least now when we explain it to them, they won't be starting from scratch.

And after all, isn't that how Spoon language started: as a way to begin a conversation on what invisible illnesses are and how they affect our lives? Not a secret language that only those who know the password and handshake can use.

Chapter Ten: Society, Sickness, and Sanity

What Is Sanity? • On the Street • All in Our Heads • Why Do They Do This? And Why Do We Allow It? • Fun's Fun. Until It Isn't. • Trigger Warning: Trigger Warning • Is Bipolar Disorder an "Invisible Illness'? • We've Got Demons in Our Heads • New Hope for Mental Illness • More "News" About Mental Health • The Scientific Tease

What Is Sanity?

AND WHO IS SANE?

These are questions you don't hear much anymore, at least outside of judicial proceedings. Even there, the phrase "guilty but mentally ill" is gaining currency. "Not guilty by reason of insanity" made people think a criminal was getting away with something. And indeed, the "insanity defense" has been misused.

We're much more comfortable talking about health and illness, concepts we all understand, than about seemingly fixed states like sanity and insanity. They sound so final. At least illness can be treated; health can improve.

Before the deluge of psychiatric labels and the *DSM*, how to tell if a person was sane or insane was a vital question. The insane were put away, in an asylum if they were poor or discreetly out of sight at home if they were wealthy.

But were all the people in asylums insane? And what kind of treatment did they receive? Investigative journalist Nellie Bly was determined to find out. Her 1887 exposé *Ten Days in a Madhouse* was a muckraking revelation.

Bly feigned amnesia and delusional fears, was reported to the police by her landlady, and declared incurably insane.

While she was at the Women's Lunatic Asylum on Blackwell's Island, she experienced cold, hunger, brutality, and no diagnosis or treatment. Several of the other inmates were, like Bly, sane by any modern standard, but poor, friendless and alone. The newspaper she worked for arranged to have Bly released, but the other women remained to be beaten, choked, starved, humiliated, not treated, and driven insane if they weren't already.

Bly's ordeal and testimony did prompt a grand jury to recommend an increase in funding of $850,000 (quite a large sum in those days) for the Department of Charities and Corrections, which oversaw asylums. It is ironic to note that the word "asylum" originally meant a place of protection, safety, or shelter. But the jury's award went mainly for better physical conditions, warmer clothes, edible food, more and better-trained nurses, rather than actual diagnosis and treatment of the women's "insanity."

The question of who is sane and how you can tell was revisited in 1973 by psychologist David Rosenhan. A professor at Stanford University, he devised a simple experiment. He sent eight volunteers, including both women and men, to psychiatric hospitals. Each person complained of hearing a voice saying three words and no other symptoms.

All, *all*, were admitted and diagnosed, most of them as schizophrenic. Afterward, the "pseudopatients" reported to their doctors and nurses that they no longer heard the voices and were sane. They remained in the psychiatric wards for an average of 19 days, beating Nellie Bly's experience by nine days. They were required to take antipsychotic drugs as a condition of their release.

Rosenhan's report, "On being sane in insane places," created quite a stir. Indignant hospital administrators claimed that their staff were actually quite adept at identifying fakes and challenged Rosenhan to repeat the experiment.

This time hospital personnel were on their guard. They identified over 40 people as being "pseudopatients" who were faking mental illness. Rosenhan, however, had sent no volunteer pseudopatients this time. It was a dismal showing for the psychiatric community.

Times have changed, of course. Few people are confined in locked wards for life. Diagnosis is, if not yet a science, less of a guessing game, backed up by the *DSM* and assorted checklists of symptoms. And insurance companies hold the keys to psychiatric units as much as medical personnel do.

Still, the fundamental questions remain. Are neurotics sane and psychotics insane? I have bipolar 2. Am I mentally ill? I would have to say I am, since my condition requires treatment, barring any dramatic scientific advances, for the rest of my life. And my illness does affect my ability to function "normally." Yet I think that few would consider me insane, unless I were suddenly to start shooting people in a public place, of course.

Speaking freely about mental illness and mental health is, presumably, supposed to make such disorders more understandable, less fearsome, less stigmatized. I suspect, however, that there are those who would rather we remained out of sight, if not locked away in asylums, then restrained in the virtual straitjackets of strong psychotropic medication.

And while group homes and other sorts of assisted living situations are now more available (though not nearly as accessible as the need for them would require), the general public prefers that such facilities, along with halfway houses for addicts and parolees, be constructed "NIMBY" – Not In My Back Yard.

Out of sight, out of mind.

Maybe the conversations surrounding such issues are reducing the stigma of mental illness, or insanity, or whatever you choose to call it, but I'm dubious about the level of success. There's still a long way to go.

On the Street

HERE'S A STORY that caught my eye recently.

Two thousand unmarked graves were found on the grounds of an old hospital. Whose could they be? Civil War dead? Victims of an epidemic?

No. That section of the old hospital was an asylum, and the bodies were those of inmates. The insane. The developmentally delayed. The rebellious. Anyone the family wanted to hide and forget.

Of course, we don't do that anymore. No more locked, back wards. No more Snake Pits. No more Cuckoo's Nests.

No, the asylums, pardon me, behavioral health residential facilities have largely been closed and the inmates, pardon me, clients or residents or patients released.

After their 30 days of insurance coverage run out.

To a group home that has a waiting list longer than the Mississippi.

To outpatient centers that hand out meds that may or may not have an effect or even be taken.

To the streets.

To a society that hates and fears them, lumps them all together as eyesores and NIMBYs, panhandlers, homeless and jobless, and spree killers.

Of course, there are mentally ill people who are able to function in society on some level or another. They're the ones who have likely never been in a locked ward. Those with understanding families, good insurance, nearby therapists, and a support system of friends. People who can hold a job. The ones who hardly ever shoot other people. People like me.

Still, the functional mental patients, your coworkers and neighbors and even family members are afraid to "come out" as needing help or getting help. They won't even admit to taking Prozac, despite it's being one of the most prescribed drugs in America.

Why is that? Because even if the asylums are gone, largely closed by lack of funding rather than obsolescence, the stigma remains. As a society, we have the impression that all people with mental disorders are psychotics or schizophrenics, lurking nearby just waiting for the chance to get their names in the papers and on TV.

We don't lock up mental patients much anymore. Now we're humane. We give them apathy, invisibility, fear, and maybe a few drugs.

And the same old stigma.

All in Our Heads

WELL, MENTAL DISORDERS probably *are* mostly in our heads, or at least our brains. And genes. I keep seeing news features that "offer hope" for new diagnostic tools and treatments that "may someday" alleviate the suffering.

Here's an example from the University of Pennsylvania:

> Many factors, both genetic and environmental, have been blamed for increasing the risk of a diagnosis of schizophrenia. Some, such as a family history of schizophrenia, are widely accepted. Others, such as infection with Toxoplasma gondii, a parasite transmitted by soil, undercooked meat and cat feces, are still viewed with skepticism. A new study used epidemiological modeling methods to determine the proportion of schizophrenia cases that may be attributable to T. gondii infection. The work suggests that about one-fifth of cases may involve the parasite.

Great. I am sure that schizophrenics will be comforted by the thought that their problems are caused by brain parasites and cat poop.

I noticed that the study showed that only 20 percent of schizophrenia "may" involve the parasite. What about the other 80 percent? Are those cases caused by some other parasite? And how will the parasites be detected? Blood test? Brain biopsy? Could be a world of horrors there for the already mentally unstable. And, perhaps most important, will real-world results back up the computer simulations?

Schizophrenia is far from the only illness being studied. Bipolar disorder and our old pal depression come in for their share of lab work too. *USA Today* recently reported on a procedure that might help with depression:

> The treatment — transcranial magnetic stimulation — was approved by the Food and Drug Administration in 2008 for the treatment of patients with medication-resistant depression.
>
> Magnets generate a directed, pulsed magnetic field — similar to an MRI in strength — to the prefrontal cortex, the front part of the brain behind the forehead. The magnetic fields induce small electrical currents, which encourage a mood-lifting chemical reaction in the brain.
>
> The treatment is daily, for four to six weeks. If the patient improves enough, the treatment is then provided as a periodic booster.

Never mind that it's entirely subjective when a patient has improved "enough" or even shows anything other than a placebo effect. And never mind the effects of having 42 MRI-strength treatments in a row.

Apparently, scientists and insurance companies are battling it out on the money front. There's a surprise.

Plus, as always, there are nay-sayers:

> The National Institute of Mental Health describes the treatment as effective for some patients, but notes that studies of its efficacy have been "mixed." The American Psychiatric Association's guidelines for depression treatment states the procedure conveys "relatively small to moderate benefits."

To the desperate, any potential "cure" or even palliative treatment eventually seems worth a try. I should know. I came *that* close (imagine several millimeters here) to having a go at electro-convulsive therapy (ECT), formerly known as shock treatment.

The thing is, you only hear about theories that "might" be correct and treatments that "may" help. Studies are hardly ever published that say, "You know that treatment we said was going to relieve the suffering of millions? Turns out, not so much." If the general public even gets to see the negative results, they may still cling to the hope offered by the earlier reports.

Just look at the anti-vaxxers. It has been repeatedly proved that childhood vaccines do not cause autism. The experiment that reported that finding was a fraud and the author, Andrew Wakefield, has been discredited, investigated and found guilty of "four counts of dishonesty and 12 involving the abuse of developmentally challenged children." Basically, he's been kicked out of medicine altogether and given the Lifetime Achievement in Quackery award by the Good Thinking Society. I'm not making that up.

And yet epidemics of measles and other deadly diseases continue to rise as parents yield to fear and refuse to have their children vaccinated.

I'm not trying to say that a parasite *doesn't* cause some cases of schizophrenia or that magnetic therapy will *never* relieve anyone's depression.

I'm just saying that if those theories are proved false, we'll likely never hear about it from the popular press.

Why Do They Do This? And Why Do We Allow It?

THE BIG STORY recently for those of us with mental disorders was this one:

A woman, Ms. Rios, was declared mentally incompetent at a hearing for a minor offense and not allowed to say goodbye to her mother. She wanted to sit on a bench and cry for a bit. When she did not go promptly with the officer, he dragged her through the courthouse by her shackled feet. A video was taken on a cellphone camera by a lawyer who happened to be present but had nothing to do with Ms. Rios's case. If you watch the video clip you can see and hear her distress.

As the headline says, this was barbaric.

But there's lots neither the headline nor the story says. I have questions.

What is the woman's mental illness? Or why is she mentally incompetent? The stories vary, usually calling her "mentally ill," which is shorter for the headline writers, but so far, I have seen nothing more specific. One could get the impression that in the mind of the media (and therefore their readers) that the two terms mean the same thing. Was she medicated or unmedicated or off her prescribed meds? Does she have a developmental disability? An autism spectrum disorder? An emotional or behavioral disorder? We don't know. But does the label make her automatically suspected of potential violence? The woman did not behave like an animal even when she was treated like one.

I think we all know people who have mental disorders but are still mentally competent to conduct their own affairs, up to and including court proceedings. In fact, I know you know one, me. But who among us, or among the sanest and most stable of the general public, wouldn't have needed to sit on a bench and cry before going to wherever the officer thought we should go? Who wouldn't yell and protest and try to hold on to a table if we were dragged anywhere by our shackled feet?

Why is the officer's action called "barbaric?" I'm not saying it wasn't barbaric. But how was it more barbaric than other things routinely done to the incarcerated mentally ill, or incompetent? Could it be because the officer's actions were caught on tape? How many everyday barbaric actions aren't? And putting aside simple human compassion, which he did, didn't the officer's actions create a larger, potentially more dangerous disturbance?

Why did the other officers present do nothing? That is evident in video taken at the time. They are spectators. No one says, "Hey, do you have to do that?" or "Give her a minute to calm down" or "Here, let me take care of this" or "You know, there are other ways to handle this" or even "Are you sure you want to do that with the camera rolling?" Nothing. Nada. Zippety. Doo-dah.

Why weren't the officers and other courthouse personnel trained to handle situations like that? They obviously happen occasionally. Officers are (supposedly) trained to handle situations involving violent felons (which Ms. Rios wasn't), domestic violence, and how to restrain suspects properly. Some even get sensitivity training on race, sexual orientation, and ethnicity. Where's the training for interacting with the mentally ill or mentally incompetent? For de-escalating a situation instead of throwing gas on the fire? How about anger management *before* incidents like this one instead of after? Shouldn't every law enforcement official be able to control or channel his or her anger and not take it out on the public?

Why the hell aren't police officers required to wear body cameras – and have someone whose job it is to, oh, I don't know, review them occasionally? Certainly, when there's been a complaint, but spot checks might also do some good. Why are civilians subject to increasing surveillance, while law enforcement personnel – *who are also civilians, by the way* – perform their jobs with minimal oversight?

And why is the Golden Rule suspended when the "others" have a mental disturbance? I'd really like to know.

Fun's Fun. Until It Isn't.

WHEN MY HUSBAND, Dan, and I were dating, he would sometimes tickle me, or poke me, or make embarrassing jokes about bodily functions. And I would shut him down. "Stop that!" in the tone of voice that says, "I mean it and I'm angry." If he persisted, I put my foot down even harder.

"You know what's wrong with you?" he would say. "You've forgotten how to have fun."

I had to admit it was partly true. I had just come off a relationship in which I could set no boundaries. Rex would tickle me, for example, past the point of enjoyment until it was actually physically painful. I taught myself to shut down my tickle response, and who knows how many other responses along with it. I was depressed, I was damaged, and I didn't know what fun looked like anymore. But I knew that for me, tickling was not it, and that I had to clamp down on it or it might turn into pain.

A Facebook post brought this all back to me. Judi, an awesome teacher of troubled teens, told of a time when a male student, "Johnny," was teasing a girl, poking and tickling her and saying he wanted to handcuff her and tickle her till she screamed.

Judi objected. She explained, "Johnny, when you say to a woman who says 'No' to you that you're going to restrain her with handcuffs and touch her without her permission until she screams, that sounds really rape-y to me."

The boy protested that he hadn't done anything wrong, and Judi took advantage of the teachable moment for a lesson on bodily autonomy: "That means you have a say in who touches you and how far you're willing to go. In my family, if someone says, 'Stop tickling,' we do, because consent is important to fun. If it's all fun for you, and not for your partner, you aren't listening to her needs."

She added, "If you don't respect her bodily autonomy when she says no tickling, or no touching, or to leave her alone, then will you respect her saying no when she doesn't want to hug, or kiss, or get it on after a date? The pattern is the same. There's the connection to rape."

As with most teachers, she had no idea whether her message had an effect.

Until later that day, when a boy from a different class started an argument with his girlfriend, and grabbed her wrist, because she wouldn't hug him.

Johnny was right there. "That ain't cool. If she doesn't want to hug right now, you got no call to get mad at her. You don't own her ass, or her. She gets to decide if she feels like hugging you, kissing you, whatever. It's called BODILY AUTONOMY, asshole. No wonder she don't want to hug you if you won't take NO for an answer!" Johnny said.

Judi thanked Johnny for listening to her and said she was proud of him. In fact, she later described this as her proudest moment of teaching all year.

Dan and I worked through our problem, I'm glad to say. I learned that I could say "no" and he learned not to push it. We both learned how to do things that were fun for both of us. Back then, I had never heard about "bodily autonomy." We learned.

I wonder if Rex ever did.

Trigger Warning: Trigger Warning

WHAT IS A trigger warning?

Let's start with a more basic question. What is a trigger?

Just as a literal trigger activates a gun, a figurative trigger activates your mental disorder. It's a stimulus that sets off either a manic or depressive phase, or a bout of PTSD.

Triggers are usually unique to the individual. What sets you off may not affect me at all.

Over the years I've learned what my triggers are, and so do most bipolar or PTSD sufferers. Loud noises and large crowds trigger my anxiety, which is why I could never work at a Chuck E. Cheese. My depressive phases don't often have triggers except for bad dreams about an ex-boyfriend. Most of my depressive episodes just happen without a trigger.

Generally, one avoids triggers, because who needs more manic or depressive phases in addition to those that occur naturally, with no prompting?

A trigger warning is something else. It is a notice that someone puts at the beginning of a piece of writing to warn readers that the subject matter may be intense. Ordinarily, trigger warnings are given for major life events that have caused trauma and may cause flashbacks, severe stress, or other extreme reactions.

Some of the most common trigger warnings are for graphic depictions of rape, suicide, self-harm, or physical or sexual abuse. The trigger warning says to a potential reader: If you don't want to encounter this material, if you think it will make your illness worse, or cause you undue stress, don't read any further.

Although we call relatively minor stimuli triggers, they usually do not require trigger warnings. If you're going to write about having a fight with your mother, you probably don't need to put a trigger warning on it. If your mother hit you in the face with a frying pan and sent you to the ER, you might need to place a trigger warning on your post about it.

Online, the standard form for trigger warnings is first to state, often in all caps, TRIGGER WARNING and state the type of trigger it is – TRIGGER WARNING: SELF-HARM, TRIGGER WARNING: SUICIDAL THOUGHTS, etc. To be extra sensitive, the writer leaves a number of blank spaces or a few dots before beginning to write the difficult material. This gives the reader the choice of whether to scroll down and read it or not.

Trigger warnings have become controversial, particularly in schools and colleges. Many pieces of literature and even textbooks on history or sociology discuss difficult topics that may be triggering. For example, a novel might feature a rape as a plot point, or a history text might discuss slavery.

Some people believe that a trigger warning will help a prospective reader know whether reading further will provoke a strong reaction. Other people believe that trigger warnings are a way of coddling the weak and letting students avoid challenging material that is necessary for the class.

My own opinion is that a trigger warning is like chicken soup: It won't hurt and might help. It may mean that a student asks for an alternative reading or assignment, but it also may mean that the student simply wants to be in a safe space (not surrounded by strangers, for example) before reading the material.

People that believe trigger warnings should not be given have usually not experienced the kind of emotional breakdown that can result from unexpectedly confronting a traumatic topic. Very likely they have never even been in the presence of someone who has had such an extreme reaction.

I suppose that ideally, we could all read any material and simply brush it off if we found it troubling. Unfortunately, for those of us with mental disorders such as bipolar illness, PTSD, and anxiety disorders, this is simply not possible. A trigger warning may prevent someone from having a public meltdown and others from having to witness one.

I don't know why that should be controversial. It seems like simple courtesy to me.

Is Bipolar Disorder an "Invisible Illness?"

YES AND NO.

First, a little on the concept of invisible illnesses. These are the sorts of afflictions that are not apparent on first looking at a person, conditions such as fibromyalgia, chronic fatigue syndrome, celiac and Crohn's diseases, diabetes, epilepsy, lupus, Lyme disease, and many others.

Disabled-world.com says, "Many people living with a hidden physical disability or mental challenge are still able to be active in their hobbies, work and be active in sports. On the other hand, some struggle just to get through their day at work and some cannot work at all."

Most mental disorders are invisible illnesses by that definition. There isn't a sign around our necks that proclaims "Bipolar," "Social Anxiety Disorder," "PTSD," "Depression," or even "Schizophrenia." The word "Crazy" isn't tattooed on our foreheads. Our mere appearance doesn't give away our "secret."

We have a lot of the same problems that people with other invisible illnesses have. Spoon theory, for example. For bipolar people, simply taking a shower requires so many spoons that we seldom go out. I count myself among that number. People who don't know or understand Spoon Theory often don't understand why we don't accept their invitations or why we cancel at the last minute, or simply don't show up. You lose a fair number of friends that way.

On the other hand, a mental disorder is not always invisible. People can see us burst into tears for no apparent reason or go into the bathroom at a party and never come out. They can see our shaking hands, confused looks, and depressed expressions. They can hear our awkward attempts to socialize "appropriately." They may not know *what* is wrong, but they can often tell *something* is.

When we realize this is happening, there are various strategies we try. We can leave the situation, entirely or partially. My go-to is to leave the room on the pretext of needing to make a cup of tea. We can try to brush it off or laugh it off: "Sorry. My nerves are bad today" or "I don't know why I said that. Must be a brain-fart." We can try the half-truth/half-joke: "Oops. Guess my meds just haven't kicked in yet." We can ignore whatever is happening and hope everyone else does too.

Or we can own it. "I have social anxiety disorder and need to be in a less crowded space than the mall." "I won't be able to go to the carnival with you because my PTSD is triggered by loud noises." "I may come to your party if my bipolar disorder will let me."

We can also address the subject when there isn't a situation looming. During a phone conversation or an IM chat, we can let the other person know that we have a mental disorder, an invisible illness. It doesn't have to be dramatic and dire. Casually may be the best way to handle it. "I know you're wondering why I didn't go to the movies with you last week." "When I saw my doctor yesterday we talked about my physical health and my mental health too." "You know that character on that show that has PTSD? I have that too, but it's not exactly like on the show."

If that sounds risky, you're right. It can be. There will be people who still don't get it. People who "don't believe in" mental illness. People who try to brush it off. People who offer the latest vitamins or super foods or Eastern philosophy as the cure-all.

But you'll also find people who say, "Oh, my brother-in-law has that too" or "Okay. But I'm still your friend" or "What can I do to help?"

So those are the choices, basically.

Take a chance. Or stay invisible.

Neither choice is right or wrong for everyone. Mental illness is very personal.

You decide.

We've Got Demons in Our Heads

THE MEDIA DON'T say it in so many words, but that's what they mean when they talk about "mental illness" after a tragedy, especially one that involves gun violence and mass murder.

Demons are responsible. And those demons are the mentally ill and/or their medications, or lack of medications. Any way you look at it, we are the demons.

Here's one of my favorite examples lately:

"It seems to me, again without having all the details about this, that these individuals have been medicated and there may be a real issue in this country from the standpoint of these drugs and how they're used."

This was from Rick Perry, *Daily Kos* reminds us, "the fellow who destroyed his last presidential bid after a bizarre debate performance that he later blamed on prescription painkillers he had taken beforehand."

Don't you love that part about speaking without having the details?

And this, from Mike Adams, who calls himself "The Health Ranger" and Editor of *NaturalNews.com*:

The headline is "Every mass shooting over last 20 years has one thing in common... and it's not guns." The article is actually a reprint of "an important article written by Dan Roberts from AmmoLand.com."

NaturalNews sounds maybe okay, but when the source is AmmoLand, you've got to wonder about bias.

Here goes:

"The overwhelming evidence points to the signal [sic] largest common factor in all of these incidents is the fact that all of the perpetrators were either actively taking powerful psychotropic drugs or had been at some point in the immediate past before they committed their crimes."

Then follows a list of people, crimes, and drug names. The list was compiled and published to Facebook by "John Noveske, founder and owner of Noveske Rifleworks just days before he was mysteriously killed in a single car accident."

Again, note the source and possible bias, plus the hint of conspiracy theory. Gotta love it.

Want something more mainstream? How about *Newsweek*?

"Charleston Massacre: Mental Illness Common Thread for Mass Shootings," by Matthew Lysiak:

".... If history is any indication, the shooter most likely has a history of severe mental health issues that have either gone untreated or undiagnosed."

He then provides a list of crimes and psychiatric diagnoses with a number of the same instances as the AmmoLand account, though not a listing of medications.

The author goes on to say that the "rise [in mass shootings] correlates directly with the closure of the mental health institutions in 1969, according to mental health experts."

Correlates with – not caused by – please note. That's important.

Lysiak goes on to say that the requirements for civil commitment *(read: involuntary)* are too loose. He quotes Liza Gold, a forensic psychiatrist in Arlington, Virginia: "The commitment requirement needs to be less strict. Today it currently requires both mental illness and dangerousness to have someone committed. I think we need to focus more on the dangerousness and keep these people from getting guns."

If that's so, we should be worried more about "sane" people such as abusive partners with histories of violence and restraining orders than about the mentally disordered, shouldn't we? Comments revealing that "most people who commit acts of violence don't exhibit signs of mental illness, and most people who are mentally ill are not violent" are buried near the end of the article.

Fortunately, not all the media are demonizing the mentally ill, though the dissent doesn't seem to be coming from the major media. *Slate* and *Salon* have published articles that question the automatic connection.

The article on *Slate*, by Anne Skomorowsky, is long, and refers to the Germanwings airplane deaths, but it's thoughtful reading and well worth the time.

"Because Germanwings pilot Andreas Lubitz killed himself when he purposefully drove a plane carrying 149 other people into a mountain in the Alps, there has been an assumption that he suffered from 'depression' — an assumption strengthened by the discovery of antidepressants in his home and reports that he had been treated in psychiatry and neurology clinics." She adds, "Lubitz did not die quietly at home. He maliciously engineered a spectacular plane crash and killed 150 people. Suicidal thoughts can be a hallmark of depression, but mass murder is another beast entirely."

And the take-away: "Many patients and other interested parties are rightly concerned that Lubitz's murderous behavior will further stigmatize the mentally ill."

Salon's Arthur Chu talked about the more recent Charleston, SC, shootings and other incidents in "It's not about mental illness: The big lie that always follows mass shootings by white males."

"I get really really tired of hearing the phrase 'mental illness' thrown around as a way to avoid saying other terms like 'toxic masculinity,' 'white supremacy,' 'misogyny' or 'racism.'

"'The real issue is mental illness' is a goddamn cop-out. I almost never hear it from actual mental health professionals, or advocates working in the mental health sphere....Seeking medical help for depression or anxiety is apparently stronger evidence of violent tendencies than going out and purchasing a weapon....Doing the former is something we're OK with stigmatizing but not the latter."

I'll let that be the last word, fellow demons. Until the next time, that is. Until the next time.

New Hope for Mental Illness

DID YOU HEAR THE NEWS?

Bullying, inflammation, anger, low self-esteem, abuse, biochemicals, unsettled gender identity, cat parasites, and anything bad causes depression/bipolar disorder/PTSD. Double-jointedness, too, except I don't know if that's bad or not.

But don't worry. Reading, happy memories, cat videos, a new vaccine, or Tylenol can help!

Science reporting these days is confusing, deceptive, and sometimes just plain wrong. Perhaps science reporters don't mean to mislead, but that's exactly what they do. Among the problems are publishing demands, lack of knowledge, logical fallacies, and the difference between correlation and causation.

Let me explain.

Publishers demand big, catchy headlines, and they prefer "New Hope for Bipolar on Your Grocer's Shelf" to "Experiments on Genes and Diseases Continue." Add to that the fact that editorial budgets have been slashed and personnel shuffled around so much that today's "science reporter" may have been last month's "political correspondent" – and trained only in basic journalism, if that.

Science is complicated and difficult to understand, unless you've got special training. Even then, your expertise is likely to be in only one area, the microbiology of prostate cancer in mice, for example. And most people's understanding of how scientific research works is, well, not understanding so much as knowing that DNA is somehow like a fingerprint.

There's a website with videos that tackle the subject quite nicely. My personal favorite is the one about animal trials in research, which explains, among other things, why my father, who had bone cancer, always said he was tired of being compared to a white rat.

Another problem is argument by analogy, which appears more in opinion pieces than in stories labeled as science. But here's a sample, damning research on psychotropic drugs, written by Kelly Brogan, MD, ABIHM (American Board of Integrative Holistic Medicine).

> The most applicable analogy is that of the woman with social phobia who finds that drinking two cocktails eases her symptoms. One could imagine how, in a 6 week randomized trial, this "treatment" could be found efficacious and recommended for daily use and even prevention of symptoms. How her withdrawal symptoms after 10 years of daily compliance could lead those around her to believe that she "needed" the alcohol to correct an imbalance. This analogy is all too close to the truth.

Well, no it's not, for a number of reasons. Analogies always break down after a while, some sooner than others. For example, that hypothetical six-week trial would be longer than six weeks, come only after years of animal studies, including ones that focused on unwanted side effects like, I don't know, hangovers or liver damage. The trial would have included control groups, placebos, and other research protocols. The ten-year "withdrawal" effect wouldn't show up in six weeks; people who drink only two drinks per day are not generally considered alcoholics or go into withdrawal, indeed they may be drinking wine for heart health.

And so forth. Having two drinks per day is *not* analogous to taking a medication for social anxiety disorder. It's associating the disliked thing (psychotropic meds) with a thing known to be bad (alcoholism) and damning by association.

Here's another flaw: the principle that "correlation does not equal causation." The classic example comes from the 1950s, when it was claimed that rock and roll music would lead to teenage pregnancies. It's true that some teenagers who listened to rock and roll became pregnant (correlation). But some didn't. And some teenagers who listened to country or jazz became pregnant. And I think by now we know what really causes pregnancy (causation).

This problem is illustrated by an article, "Scientists: The 'Tortured Artist' Is a Real Thing." The first thing to notice is that the headline is misleading, or possibly completely untrue. The article explains a study that supposedly shows that "creative genius and mental disorders are connected at a genetic level," then goes on to debunk it:

> "Any particular set of genes is only going to explain a very small part of variation in any psychological trait," says Scott Barry Kaufman, a psychologist at the University of Pennsylvania. Indeed, the variants in the new study have a tiny, miniscule impact on creativity – less than 1 percent.

The rest of the article waffles back and forth and concludes inconclusively. Are creativity and "madness" linked somehow? Possibly. Does one cause the other? We don't know, but there are a lot of theories. There are lots of other possible factors. Without the headline, would anyone read that? How do you define "creativity," anyway?

Here's a selection of recent articles that purport to have some relevance to mental illness or mental health.

Can Reading Make You Happier?
Answer: Bibliotherapy helps some people, possibly because of changes in the brain.

Artificial Recreation Of Happy Memories May Become The Next Big Weapon Against Depression
Thesis: "Urging a depressed person to stay positive by remembering the good things in life is unlikely to be helpful advice. That is because depression blocks access to happy memories. But what if we could somehow artificially recreate such memories to allow for some more positive thinking? A study suggests that this is indeed possible – at least in rats....However, more research will be necessary to obtain a clearer picture of how this might work in humans." *(Again with the rats.)*

Science Shows that Watching Cat Videos is Good for You
The article, which says "research suggests that the pleasure you derive from watching cat videos can often outweigh the guilt of procrastination," is largely tongue-in-cheek, but that headline is a grabber. Headlines that use "waffle words" like *may, can, might, possibly, someday, appears to* usually indicate a story that says nothing significant. They build up hope, but if a study comes along that disproves the theory, it will never be reported. (http://www.iflscience.com/environment/science-shows-watching-cat-videos-good-you)

Researchers Are Developing A Vaccine For Post-Traumatic Stress Disorder
It begins: "New studies are suggesting a link between the immune system and the way the body reacts to stress.

Research with rodents are raising hopes that one day, tweaking a person's immune system could be a way to treat or even prevent conditions like PTSD, *Nature* reports." How many warning signs can you spot there?

Double-Jointedness Is Linked to Anxiety
One of my favorites. Correlation/causation much?

Your pain reliever may also be diminishing your joy
Actually it says that acetaminophen blunts both positive and negative emotions. And, it adds, "this study offers support to a relatively new theory that says that common factors may influence how sensitive we are to both the bad as well as the good things in life." Gee, who would have guessed?

Is Depression a Mental or Physical Illness? Unravelling the Inflammation Hypothesis
This is actually a good article. The headline question is a valid and interesting one, and the author states, "But while there may be a connection between inflammation and depression, one doesn't necessarily lead to the other. So it's too simplistic to say depression is a physical, rather than a psychiatric, illness." Hooray for correlation/causation!

What does all this reporting prove? Almost nothing. Except "let the reader beware."

More "News" About Mental Health

NEXT IN MY ongoing series of posts about news stories that bear on mental health, and what they may or may not mean:

Depression Damages Parts of the Brain, Research Concludes, July 2, 2015, by Sasha Petrova:

"Brain damage is caused by persistent depression rather than being a predisposing factor for it, researchers have finally concluded after decades of unconfirmed hypothesising," the article begins.
"A study published in *Molecular Psychiatry*... has proved once and for all that recurrent depression shrinks the hippocampus – an area of the brain responsible for forming new memories – leading to a loss of emotional and behavioural function."
The article also claims that "the effects of depression on the brain are reversible with the right treatment for the individual," though what those treatments might be is not explained.
The take-away: Depression damages the brain, not the other way around. What this means for patients is not yet known.

Link Found Between Gut Bacteria and Depression, July 28, 2015, by Caroline Reid

Well, if it's not the hippocampus, it might be your guts. According to this article, "Scientists have shown for the first time that there is a way to model how the gut bacteria in a mouse can have an active role in causing anxiety and depressive-like behaviors....

"[T]he lead author of the study... concluded that stress shortly after birth in mice, alongside the microbiome associated with stress, can lead to depression later in life."

The take-away: More help for depressed mice. As the study author says, "It would be interesting to see if this relationship also effects humans. ....We need to obtain some human data to be able to say with confidence that bacteria are really inducing anxiety or depression.... However, so far, the data is missing." In other words, more theory, more mice, no help for patients.

Mad Cow Disease Protein May Play a Role in Depression, by Justine Alford

"In all likelihood, there is no single cause, but one of the leading ideas is that it results from an imbalance of chemicals in the brain, namely the 'happy' hormone serotonin and the 'pleasure' hormone dopamine." Hard to argue with that. But here's the meat of the article: "[S]cientists may have just discovered another contributing factor – abnormal bundles of proteins called prions." Prions are also the culprit in mad cow disease. After some theorizing and mouse research, "the researchers propose a possible mechanism for the involvement of prion proteins in depression."

The take-away: Interesting to scientists, but no help yet for depression sufferers. Plus, the article is a bit too technical for the lay audience – and all theory, except perhaps for the mice.

Picky Eaters May Be More Likely to Develop Anxiety and Depression, by Hannah Keyser

This sums it up nicely: "The study... found that picky eaters are more likely to develop anxiety, depression, and ADHD in later years....While moderate cases were associated with symptoms of separation anxiety and ADHD, severe picky eaters were more likely to have an actual diagnosis of depression or social anxiety in later years. But the scientists stressed that this is a case of correlation, not causation."

The take-away: So, no news here. Correlation does not equal causation means this may be a coincidence, or anxiety and depression may cause picky eating, or some other factor may cause them both. Note the "May Be" in the article title – it often signals a result of little or no value.

A Urine Test Could Distinguish Between Bipolar Disorder and Depression, August 8, 2015, by Stephen Luntz

"An easy and reliable method of distinguishing bipolar disorder from major depressive disorder could save tens of thousands of lives, and transform millions more. Now researchers at Chongqing Medical University, China, claim to have found just that in a study based on biomarkers in urine." According to the study, the presence of six metabolites in urine was 90 percent reliable in diagnosing the two conditions, which are notoriously difficult to tell apart. "Studies have found that as many as 39% of patients diagnosed with MDD have unrecognized bipolar."

The take-away: More research needed, but this could be big. Pee on a stick and find out whether you're bipolar, instead of relying on the DSM. (Full disclosure: I was diagnosed with major depression for decades before my bipolar 2 diagnosis.)

The Startup That Wants to Cure Social Anxiety, by Robinson Meyer

This is, if not new, at least a little different: Cognitive Behavioral Therapy (CBT) delivered on the web. The article claims that "[R]esearch conducted over the past half-decade shows that CBT delivered via a website can be just as effective as CBT delivered through an in-person therapist." The service, called "Joyable," can be accessed for $99 per month or $239 for three months, which includes a coach. The company says that the online treatment "reduces the stigma around seeking out therapy."

The take-away: Yeah. We'll see. And lose the name "Joyable," for heaven's sake. (Full disclosure: I've never been a fan of CBT.)

Cats and Mental Health, Mental Health Foundation

Survey says, "Half of those people [more than 600 individuals surveyed in 2011] described themselves as having a mental health problem. The results highlighted some of the benefits of feline ownership:

- 87% of cat owners feel that the animals have a positive impact on their wellbeing
- 76% find that coping with everyday life is easier thanks to the animals
- Stroking a cat is a calming and helpful activity."

The article also refutes the myth about "crazy cat ladies" and self-harm.

My take-away: Pet therapy is a recognized technique that provides benefits to shut-ins, geriatric and psychiatric patients, those with ADD and autism, and even prisoners.

My four cats increase the effects of Zoloft, Ativan, Lamictal, and Abilify. Be sure to have your pet spayed or neutered.

The Scientific Tease

I KNOW THE headlines and accompanying news stories are supposed to give us hope: New Treatments for Mentally Ill, Scientific Advances for PTSD Suffers, How Research Is Finding Causes, – and Possible Cures, – for Bipolar Disorder, Brain Science May Explain OCD.

But the reality is that those headlines are teasers. Once you read the story, you realize how little is new, how far from reality the science is, and how long it will be until the supposed cures make any difference.

But drugs aren't all the scientific world is offering for people with bipolar and other mental disorders. There are transcranial stimulators, magnets, fMRI, and other technologies that hold promise for at least understanding our illnesses and, in some cases, treating them. Studies of the human brain, DNA, epigenetics, neurotransmitters, precursor chemicals, and more are touted as ways to unravel the mysteries of why some people get mental illnesses and some don't; why some medications work for some people and not for others; and how the medications that actually do work do what they do.

If you are buoyed by the hope these scientific articles and the advances they hold out, you may envision a world in which parents can tell when a baby is liable to depression and watch for early signs; a troubled teen can be diagnosed with bipolar 1, 2, or psychotic bipolar; which particular "cocktail" of drugs is the best fit for an individual; how a small machine can send signals to the brain that will ease the symptoms of, well, anything.

Unfortunately, that's not true. Oh, there is scientific research going on, although there would be more if funding for mental health issues were taken more seriously. But not all that research will result in effective, practical treatments for mental illness, more closely targeted drugs, new understandings of various psychological models, new methods of diagnosis. A breakthrough, when it comes, may even be discovered as an unexpected side effect of something else entirely.

Besides, can you imagine these wonder drugs and diagnostic tools, and nanobot treatments (or whatever) making it to the vast majority of the mentally ill? Will psychologists be able to send clients to get an fMRI to pinpoint problems, and will the insurance pay for that? How would you convince a homeless schizophrenic to place his head in that clanking machine, hold still for half an hour, and answer questions? How long will it take the FDA to study and approve a new drug, and will it cost $12,000 or more per year? And will insurance coverage even be available because it's still considered "experimental"?

Frankly, I can't see most of these heralded miracle treatments making their way down to the community mental health center level anytime soon, even once they've been developed, tested, proven, and put on the market. Like so much of medicine, I fear psychiatric advances will be available only to the rich or those with platinum-level insurance. And although one in four Americans will experience some form of mental illness in their lifetimes – and millions more friends, relatives, caregivers, and loved ones will be affected by it as well, psychiatric topics don't draw government or university funding or charitable support the way other conditions like HIV, breast cancer, and heart disease do.

So, forgive me if I see those uplifting headlines and think, "Pfft. More pie in the sky." I do think progress is being made and will continue to be made, but I doubt whether it will be soon enough, or tested enough, or cheap enough, or available enough to benefit me. You younger folks, now – you may still reap the benefits of these remarkable advances. But in the meantime, while you're waiting for that magic pill or Star Trek device, keep on taking the meds you've been prescribed, and talking to your psychotherapist, and building a support system, and taking care of yourself.

For now, let's work with what we've got.

www.ingramcontent.com/pod-product-compliance
Lightning Source LLC
Chambersburg PA
CBHW030106100526
44591CB00009B/290